Word Skills & Vocabulary Grades 4-

D1300315

Turn to each section to find a more detailed skills list.

Table of Contents

What Does This Book Include?

- More than 75 student practice pages that reinforce basic word skills and vocabulary
- A detailed skills list for each section of the book
- Send-home letters that inform parents of the skills being targeted and ways to practice these skills
- Student checkups
- Reproducible student progress charts
- Awards to celebrate student progress
- Answer keys for easy checking
- Perforated pages for easy removal and filing if desired

What Are the Benefits of This Book?

- Organized for quick and easy use
- Enhances and supports your existing reading and writing programs
- Offers multiple practice opportunities
- Helps develop mastery of basic skills
- Provides reinforcement for different ability levels
- Includes communication pages that encourage parents' participation in their children's learning of reading and writing
- Contains checkups that assess students' word skills and vocabulary knowledge
- Offers reproducible charts for documenting student progress
- Aligns with national literacy standards

How to Use This Book
Steps to Success

Choose Skills to Target

Scan the detailed table of contents at the beginning of each section to find just the right skills to target your students' needs.

Select Fun Practice Pages

Choose from a variety of fun formats the pages that best match your students' current ability levels.

Fun Formats

Date Skill Completed

Targeted Skill

Letter to Parents Informing Them of Skill to Review

Communicate With Parents

Recruit parent assistance by locating the appropriate parent letter (pages 102–124), making copies, and sending the letter home.

Problems for Practice

Skills Review for Parents

Assess Student Understanding

Assess students' progress with student checkups (mini tests) on pages 103–125. Choose Checkup A or Checkup B.

Checkup 1

Name _____ Date _____

Use the word bank to write a synonym for each word.

1. postpone _____ 2. divide _____
3. donate _____ 4. steal _____

Use the word bank to write an antonym for each word.

5. buy _____ 6. simple _____
7. east _____ 8. crooked _____

Use the word bank to write one synonym and one antonym for each word.

9. alike_____ _____
10. ask_____ _____

straight	give	question	same
delay	west	different	answer
sell	split	complex	take

Test A: Synonyms and antonyms

103

Checkup 1

Name _____ Date _____

Use the word bank to write a synonym for each word.

1. quick _____ 2. bad _____
3. scare _____ 4. empty _____

Use the word bank to write an antonym for each word.

5. shaky _____ 6. interesting _____
7. fail _____ 8. together _____

Use the word bank to write one synonym and one antonym for each word.

9. under _____ _____
10. listen _____ _____

steady	awful	rapid	apart
boring	above	hear	ignore
vacant	terrify	below	pass

Test B: Synonyms and antonyms

Two Checkups for Each Skill

Document Progress

Documenting student progress can be as easy as 1, 2, 3! Do the following for each student:

1. Make a copy of the Student Progress Charts (pages 126–127).
2. File the charts in his math portfolio or a class notebook.
3. Record the date each checkup is given, the number of correct answers, and any comments regarding his progress.

Student Progress Chart

student		Date	Number Correct	Comments
Checkup 1 Synonyms and Antonyms	A			
	B			
Checkup 2 Homophones	A			
	B			
Checkup 3 Easily Confused Words	A			
	B			
Checkup 4 Multiple-Meaning Words	A			
	B			
Checkup 5 Prefixes	A			
	B			
Checkup 6 Suffixes	A			
	B			

126

Celebrate!

Celebrate word skills and vocabulary success using the awards on page 101.

Great aim!

_____ student _____
is right on target with
_____ skill _____
_____ teacher _____
_____ date _____

You hit the bull's-eye!

_____ student _____
hit the mark with
_____ skill _____
_____ teacher _____
_____ date _____

101

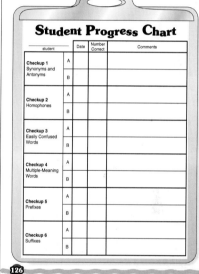

Books in the Target Reading & Writing Success series:

- *Mechanics, Grammar, & Usage* • Grs. 2–3
- *Mechanics, Grammar, & Usage* • Grs. 4–5
- *Word Skills & Vocabulary* • Grs. 2–3
- *Word Skills & Vocabulary* • Grs. 4–5

Managing Editor: Debra Liverman

Editorial Team: Becky S. Andrews, Kimberley Bruck, Karen P. Shelton, Diane Badden, Cayce Guiliano, Debra Liverman, Lauren E. Cox, Sherry McGregor, Karen A. Brudnak, Sarah Hamblet, Hope Rodgers, Dorothy C. McKinney, Kelli L. Gowdy, Elizabeth H. Lindsay, Kim Minafo

Production Team: Lisa K. Pitts, Pam Crane, Clevell Harris, Rebecca Saunders, Jennifer Tipton Bennett, Chris Curry, Theresa Lewis Goode, Ivy L. Koonce, Clint Moore, Greg D. Rieves, Barry Slate, Donna K. Teal, Tazmen Carlisle, Amy Kirtley-Hill, Kristy Parton, Debbie Shoffner, Cathy Edwards Simrell, Lynette Dickerson, Mark Rainey

www.themailbox.com

Manufactured in the United States
10 9 8 7 6 5 4 3 2

Synonyms and Antonyms

Synonyms and Antonyms

Table of Contents

Parent Communication and Student Checkups

See pages 102–103 for corresponding parent communications and student checkups (mini tests) for synonyms and antonyms.

Banking With Birds

Name _____ Date _____

Use the word bank to write a synonym for each word.
Write the matching letter in the box.

Word Bank

wealth (T)
mend (A)
split (S)
delay (T)
illegal (K)
ache (H)
move (T)
pointed (I)
secure (R)
use (O)
entire (E)
grow (E)
untidy (N)
revise (K)
attempt (R)
take (M)

1. transport
_____

2. repair
_____

3. postpone
_____

4. change
_____

5. sharp
_____

6. develop
_____

7. unlawful
_____

8. divide
_____

9. fortune
_____

10. safe
_____

11. messy
_____

12. steal
_____

13. pain
_____

14. whole
_____

15. operate
_____

16. try
_____

Where do birds invest their money?

To solve the riddle, match each boxed letter to the numbered lines below.

___ ___   ___ ___ ___   " ___ ___ ___ ___ ___ "
5 11   1 13 6   8 3 15 10 4

___ ___ ___ ___ ___ ___ !
12 2 16 7 14 9

Sunken Treasure

Name _____ Date _____

Write a synonym for each word.
Use the word bank.

1. mistake
_____

2. follow
_____

3. disappear
_____

4. increase
_____

5. delete
_____

6. frequently
_____

7. smell
_____

Word Bank

FISH FLAKES

Fish Food

give		usual
terrify		vary
wild	omit	vacant
need	odor	depart
error	obey	raise
vanish		often

8. require
_____

9. common
_____

10. leave
_____

11. scare
_____

12. donate
_____

13. empty
_____

14. untamed
_____

15. change
_____

Jelly Bean Bandits

Name _____   Date _____

Find four synonyms for each underlined word.
Color by the code.

Color Code

said = orange   good = red
cold = purple   big = yellow
fast = blue   small = green

swift

huge

enormous

splendid

nippy

told

voiced

chilly

petite

speedy

large

little

gigantic

wonderful

icy

quick

tiny

excellent

remarked

fine

rapid

stated

undersize

frigid

Synonyms: overused words

Cool Treats

Name _____ Date _____

Color the word that is *not* a synonym.
The colored boxes lead to Roscoe's treat.

Feature Flavor Cowabunga Crunch

Lola's Ice-Cream Creations

1. mad	calm	angry	furious	upset
2. easy	basic	old	simple	plain
3. thin	skinny	sharp	slim	slender
4. walk	examine	stroll	march	trek
5. bad	awful	scare	terrible	poor
6. take	snatch	get	obey	grab
7. old	antique	used	worn	angry
8. new	modern	current	recent	terrible
9. quiet	silent	hushed	sharp	soundless
10. ask	inquire	question	give	quiz
11. wet	soaked	calm	soggy	moist
12. hot	rapid	sizzling	fiery	heated

Synonyms: overused words

Hogwash!

Write an antonym for each word.
Use the word bank.

blunt	true	bitter	cry	depart

repair	lose	buy	simple	enemy

dislike	fail	rough	enter	disobey

Word Bank

gain	laugh	sell
break	smooth	sharp
exit	pass	arrive
false	admire	complex
sweet	obey	friend

Where Are the Fish?

Name _____ Date _____

Write an antonym for each word on the puzzle.

Across
3. deep
7. earn
8. alike
10. raise
12. poor
14. fact
16. finish
17. cowardly
19. whole
20. sharp

Down
1. love
2. dangerous
4. dead
5. narrow
6. east
7. crooked
9. remember
10. early
11. play
13. old
15. loose
18. child

Just "Beach-y"

Name _____ Date _____

Write an antonym above each crossed off word.

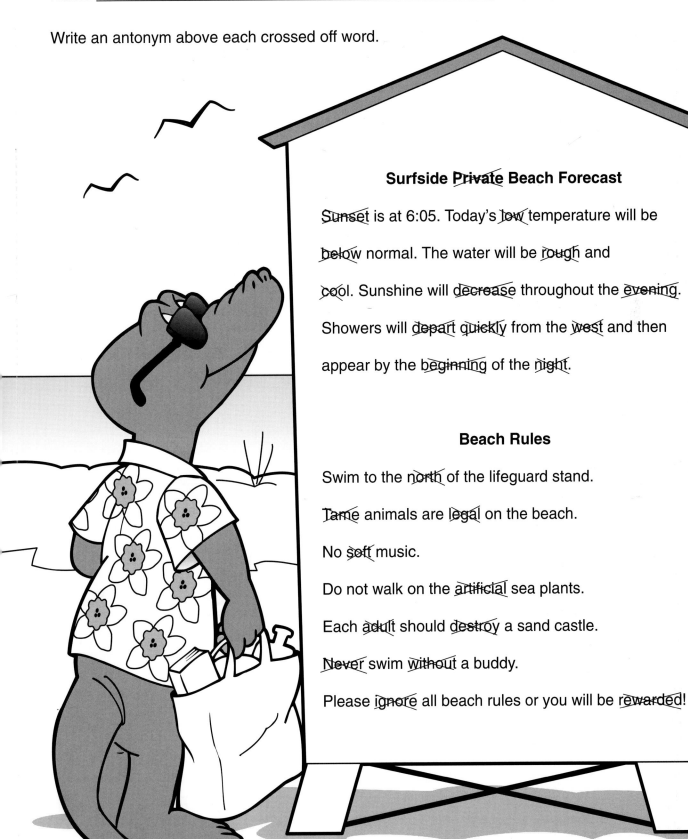

Surfside ~~Private~~ Beach Forecast

~~Sunset~~ is at 6:05. Today's ~~low~~ temperature will be ~~below~~ normal. The water will be ~~rough~~ and ~~cool~~. Sunshine will ~~decrease~~ throughout the ~~evening~~. Showers will ~~depart~~ ~~quickly~~ from the ~~west~~ and then appear by the ~~beginning~~ of the ~~night~~.

Beach Rules

Swim to the ~~north~~ of the lifeguard stand.

~~Tame~~ animals are ~~legal~~ on the beach.

No ~~soft~~ music.

Do not walk on the ~~artificial~~ sea plants.

Each ~~adult~~ should ~~destroy~~ a sand castle.

~~Never~~ swim ~~without~~ a buddy.

Please ~~ignore~~ all beach rules or you will be ~~rewarded~~!

Butter Me Up!

Name _____ Date _____

Write the antonym for each word.
Use the word bank.

dry
_____

few
_____

kind
_____

enormous
_____

collect
_____

graceful
_____

permanent
_____

follower
_____

ordinary
_____

interesting
_____

disliked
_____

whisper
_____

shaky
_____

together
_____

antique
_____

rarely
_____

idle
_____

divide
_____

POPCORN

Word Bank

steady	tiny	alone	combine	new	clumsy
many	temporary	damp	often	shout	popular
boring	scatter	leader	busy	cruel	unique

Shoe Sale

Color each word pair by the code.

Code
synonym = blue
antonym = red

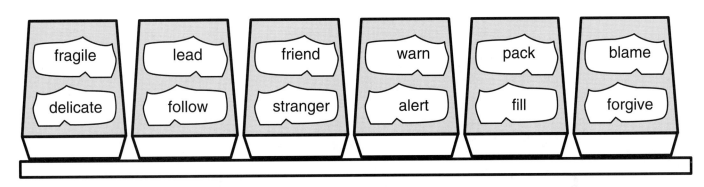

| fragile | lead | friend | warn | pack | blame |
| delicate | follow | stranger | alert | fill | forgive |

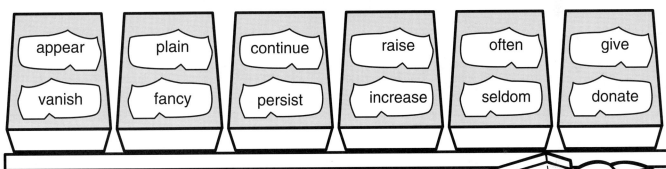

| appear | plain | continue | raise | often | give |
| vanish | fancy | persist | increase | seldom | donate |

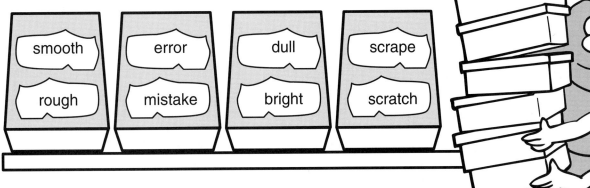

| smooth | error | dull | scrape |
| rough | mistake | bright | scratch |

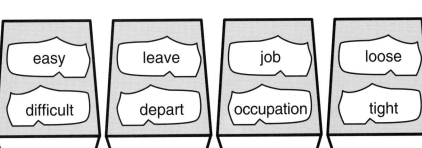

| easy | leave | job | loose |
| difficult | depart | occupation | tight |

Burger Barn

Name _____   Date _____

Write a synonym for the word on the top burger bun.
Write an antonym for the word on the bottom burger bun.
Use the word bank.

below	clean	end	love
hear	add	take	fix
healthy	quiet	late	nothing
different	glad	question	sour

Word Bank

above
adore
answer
ask
beginning
break
combine
dirty
diverse
early
everything
finish
give
grab
happy
hate
ignore
ill
listen
noisy
none
repair
sad
same
silent
sweet
spotless
subtract
tardy
tart
under
well

Synonyms and antonyms

Using the Right Word

Using the Right Word

Table of Contents

Parent Communication and Student Checkups

See pages 104–107 for corresponding parent communications and student checkups (mini tests) for homophones and easily confused words.

Blackbeak's Bounty

Name _____ Date _____

Write the homophone for each word.

1. sighed _____

2. would _____

3. eye _____

4. poor _____

5. flu _____

6. daze _____

7. new _____

8. sea _____

9. knight _____

10. allowed _____

11. break _____

12. pairs _____

Use one word from each pair to complete the paragraph.

A few _____ ago, Blackbeak found a treasure chest that had washed in from the _____. Blackbeak _____ there _____ be a big bounty inside. He worked all _____ to pull it out of the water. When he finally pulled it out, he found that it was locked.

Blackbeak said _____, "_____ can use my strong beak to _____ the lock!" The chest _____ open and Blackbeak gazed inside. The chest was filled with sweet, juicy _____.

Blackbeak _____ and said, "Well, I'm still _____, but I won't go hungry!"

A Pretty Perplexed Prince

Name _____ Date _____

Color the lily pad with the correct word to reveal the
path to the chosen princess.

1. Prince Pat has a _____-mile hop to Bog Castle.

2. He uses a map to decide _____ he is going.

3. The _____ ahead is long and hilly.

4. Prince Pat hopes _____ get to the castle on time.

5. Prince Pat must choose a princess to _____.

6. Pat has a 14-_____ gold ring for his bride.

7. The sun's hot _____ beat down on Pat as he hops.

8. Finally, Prince Pat _____ the three princesses.

9. Princess Fifi hopes Pat has the _____ to choose her.

10. Fifi, Felice, and Freida are doing _____ best to impress Pat.

11. Prince Pat and his princess will _____ over the entire bog.

12. Prince Pat hopes that he will make the _____ choice.

for	four	fore
where	ware	wear
road	rode	rowed
heal	he'll	heel
merry	Mary	marry
carrot	caret	carat
raise	rays	raze
seas	sees	seize
sense	cents	scents
their	they're	there
rein	reign	rain
rite	write	right

Princess Freida   Princess Fifi   Princess Felice

Homophones

Grover's Goof

Name _____   Date _____

Circle the incorrect homophone in each sentence.
Write the correct homophone on the matching line below.

1. Grover Gopher thought it was a grate day to learn how to play golf.

2. His first problem was deciding not to higher a golf professional.

3. He simply dressed in golfing close and went to the golf course.

4. He placed his feat so they lined up with the hole.

5. Grover guest that all he had to do was hit the ball.

6. With a loud grown, he aimed at the ball and swung his club.

7. Grover watched the ball to see witch way it went.

8. He knew it didn't go strait!

9. It wasn't hard for Grover to here a loud thud as the ball hit a tree.

10. The ball just missed hitting a hair that was hopping across the grass.

11. Grover decided that learning to play golf would take a lot of patients.

12. He'll be sure to sign up for a lessen before he plays next week!

Fore
Four!

1. _____   5. _____   9. _____

2. _____   6. _____   10. _____

3. _____   7. _____   11. _____

4. _____   8. _____   12. _____

Pachyderm Picnic

Name _____ Date _____

If the boldfaced word is used correctly, color the cookie.
If the boldfaced word is not used correctly, write the correct homophone above it.

You're Invited!

(B) Come **won,** come all

(S) To Pack E. Derm **Peak**

(O) For a **reel** picnic

(N) That cannot be **beet!**

(Q) Be **there** by two,

(T) Or even ten past the **our.**

(U) I hope the **sun** shines

(R) So we can **sea** from the tower.

(A) Your favorite **sweet** treat

(R) Is what **ewe** should bring.

(I) A **guessed** will be welcome,

(M) Just **knot** a creepy, crawly thing!

(S) This gathering will be **great**

(L) **Fore** all of our kin.

(P) I hope **yule** all come!

(H) Love, **Aunt** Gray Skin

What game do elephants play with ants?

To answer the riddle, write the letters from the colored cookies in order on the lines below.

___ ___ ___ ___ ___ ___ ___

Polly's Polar Diner

Name _____ Date _____

Color the homophone that matches the definition on the cup.
Use the other homophone in a sentence about Polly's Polar Diner.

blue   blew

the color of the sky

_____
_____
_____

maid   made

a female servant

_____
_____
_____

bored   board

a flat piece of wood

_____
_____
_____

creek   creak

a small, winding stream

_____
_____
_____

weak   week

a period of seven days

_____
_____
_____

meat   meet

to get together

_____
_____
_____

you're   your

contraction of *you are*

_____
_____
_____

knows   nose

the part of the body
used for breathing air

_____
_____
_____

Gone Fishing

Name _____ Date _____

Complete each sentence using words from the fish below.
Color each fish after using its word.

1. On the _____ Sunday in March, Percy went
   _____ on a fishing trip.

2. He wondered _____ or not the _____
   would be nice.

3. The morning _____ was heavy, and Percy worried
   that he had _____ the best fishing spot.

4. Once he made it _____ the weeds, Percy _____
   out his anchor.

5. Percy was _____ sure about the _____ he had
   tied in his fishing line.

6. He _____ as he tossed his line over the _____
   of his boat.

7. "_____ a big one!" Percy shouted as the fish took
   _____ second bite.

8. By the time he _____ the fish, he was ready to find a
   _____ and take a nap.

9. Percy's fish weighed _____ pounds, and Percy proudly
   _____ the whole thing!

forth • it's • ate • side • weather • eight

threw • cot • missed • knot • fourth • whether

mist • its • not • through • caught • sighed

Ready for the Rodeo!

Name _____ Date _____

Write the homophone that correctly completes each sentence.
Cross out the word in the lasso after using it.

Their	their	their	their	their
There	there	there	there	there
They're	they're	They're	they're	they're

1. If the rodeo begins at noon, what time should we get _____?

2. The fans are lining up. _____ all ready for the show to begin!

3. It looks as if many fans have brought _____ cameras.

4. _____ are bulls here that weigh more than 2,000 pounds!

5. The program states that _____ are rodeos in Australia.

6. The cowboys and cowgirls are here, and _____ ready to perform.

7. The judges have _____ stopwatches ready to use.

8. _____ going to time most of the rodeo events.

9. The ring is empty, but the contestants will be out _____ soon.

10. The rodeo clowns are funny, but _____ really protecting the cowboys.

11. _____ painted faces and baggy clothes distract the bulls from fallen cowboys.

12. How do cowboys keep _____ hats on while they are riding?

13. I guess they don't. Both of those cowboys lost _____ hats.

14. The hats are lying right _____ by the fence post.

15. I wonder whether _____ going to announce the winners soon.

It's a Jungle Out There!

Name _____ Date _____

If the boldfaced word is used correctly, color the banana in the yes column.
If the boldfaced word is used incorrectly, color the banana in the no column.

Yes	No
I	K
E	T
O	B
E	C
M	G
L	F
T	O
I	U
Z	C
I	S
D	N
K	P
Y	R
E	N
G	L

1. **It's** so boring to live in this jungle!

2. How can you say **its** boring? You live in a jungle!

3. The jungle is colorful, and **it's** full of bananas.

4. **It's** like having a grocery store in your own home.

5. What about **it's** pesky insects and scary animals?

6. The jungle and **its** insects and animals aren't boring.

7. **It's** not the animals or the insects that are boring.

8. If **its** not the animals or insects, is it the bananas?

9. Look at that tree. **It's** bananas are ripe and perfect.

10. **It's** not the bananas. I love bananas.

11. Is it the birds? Look at that one. **It's** feathers are yellow.

12. **It's** not the birds either. I'm just tired of hanging around.

13. Maybe **it's** just the jungle I'm tired of.

14. The jungle is alive, you know. **It's** ears are always listening.

15. If that is true, then **its** really time for me to move!

How do you make a monkey laugh?
To solve the riddle, match the colored letters above to the numbered lines below.

___ ___ ___   ___ ___ ___ ___ ___ ___   ___ ___!
13 3   8   7   1   9   12 6   4   10 2

©The Education Center, Inc. • *Target Reading & Writing Success* • TEC60877 • Key p. 129

Homophones

X Marks the Spot

Name _____ Date _____

Circle the word in parentheses that correctly completes the sentence.

1. Captain Pauly gathered his crew (all together, altogether) for a meeting.

2. He asked the skipper to please (close, clothes) the door.

3. Pauly was more excited (than, then) ever before!

4. (Accept, Except) I do remember the time he told us about a lost treasure of gold.

5. He said, "We've been unlucky for (all together, altogether) too long."

6. He continued, "I will not (accept, except) any more excuses!"

7. Pauly held up a treasure map and (than, then) we all gasped.

8. We were all curious (accept, except) Pauly.

9. Skipper said, "Tonight we will gather (all together, altogether) to make a plan."

10. He continued, "(Than, Then) tomorrow we will set sail to get this loot!"

11. We huddled (close, clothes) together and got to work.

12. Then we dressed in our treasure-hunting (close, clothes) and set sail.

13. We were ready to (accept, except) the challenge of the day.

14. Skipper yelled from above, "We're getting (close, clothes)!"

15. "We found it! Pauly shouted. "It's even better (than, then) I thought!"

©The Education Center, Inc. • *Target Reading & Writing Success* • TEC60877 • Key p. 129

"Egg-citing" Competition

Name _____ Date _____

Color the egg with the word that correctly completes each sentence.

	quit / quite
1. The chickens were in _____ a flutter the morning of the contest.	quit / quite
2. With all these chickens together, it certainly wasn't _____ !	quit / quiet
3. It was time to _____ chattering and get ready to go.	quit / quiet
4. After combing their feathers, they were _____ to go.	all ready / already
5. They were running late, and others were _____ getting started.	all ready / already
6. Charlotte was sure she could _____ the most eggs today.	lay / lie
7. She had _____ won the contest two years in a row!	all ready / already
8. She just can't _____!	lose / loose
9. It would be such a _____ for her if she did.	loss / lose
10. Charlotte said she would _____ laying eggs forever if she lost.	quit / quiet
11. Charlene said that she was being _____ dramatic.	quit / quite
12. Charlotte told her to go _____ down and leave her alone.	lay / lie
13. The crowd got _____ as the winner was announced.	quite / quiet
14. Charlotte acted surprised and said, "Is it over _____?"	all ready / already
15. Her first-place ribbon was coming _____, so she retied it.	lose / loose
16. She smiled proudly and said she would never _____ laying eggs.	quit / quite

Easily confused words

Dining Dalmatians

Name _____   Date _____

If the boldfaced word is used correctly, color the bowl.
If the boldfaced word is not used correctly, write the correct word above it.

1. **H**
Please **take** some water to me at my table.

2. **R**
Bring the dirty dishes to me.

3. **I**
I ordered banana-flavored bones for **desert.**

4. **O**
Are those chewies really that **good**?

5. **T**
Did you **bring** your owner to that restaurant?

6. **S**
Would you please **take** me a fresh napkin?

7. **P**
I will eat **desert** before dinner!

8. **O**
This soup is as hot as the **dessert** in July!

9. **T**
You did a **well** job eating all of your dinner!

10. **E.**
I ate so much I am afraid I don't feel **well.**

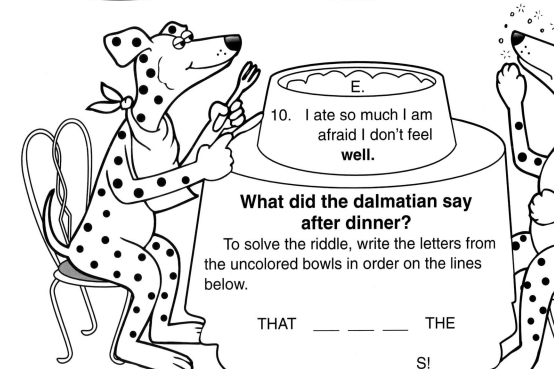

What did the dalmatian say after dinner?
To solve the riddle, write the letters from the uncolored bowls in order on the lines below.

THAT ___ ___ ___ THE

___ ___ ___ ___ S!

Puzzled Princess

Name _____ Date _____

Use the word bank to complete the puzzle.

Where is my prince?

Down

1. My mom went to _____ down.
2. We had pie for _____.
4. My baby sister is an _____!
6. My school _____ looks great!
7. My tooth is coming _____.
8. Please _____ down your books.
9. Is it eight o'clock _____?
10. I _____ the team today.
12. I'm taller _____ she is.
14. Please _____ a book to Mom.
17. We _____ our favorites last night.

Across

3. Fill the _____ with water.
5. Please _____ the door.
9. Class, clap your hands _____.
11. It's so hot that I can hardly _____.
13. It is very _____ in the library.
15. A right _____ is 90 degrees.
16. Did you _____ the gift from him?
18. Which flavor will you _____?

Word Bank

angel	angle
pitcher	picture
dessert	desert
close	clothes
all together	altogether
loose	lose
set	sit
breathe	breath
all ready	already
than	then
accept	except
chose	choose
quit	quiet
take	bring

Multiple-
Meaning
Words

Multiple-Meaning Words
Table of Contents

Parent Communication and Student Checkups

See pages 108–109 for corresponding parent communications and student checkups (mini tests) for multiple-meaning words.

Double Bubble Bath

Name _____ Date _____

Write the word from the word bank that matches both meanings.

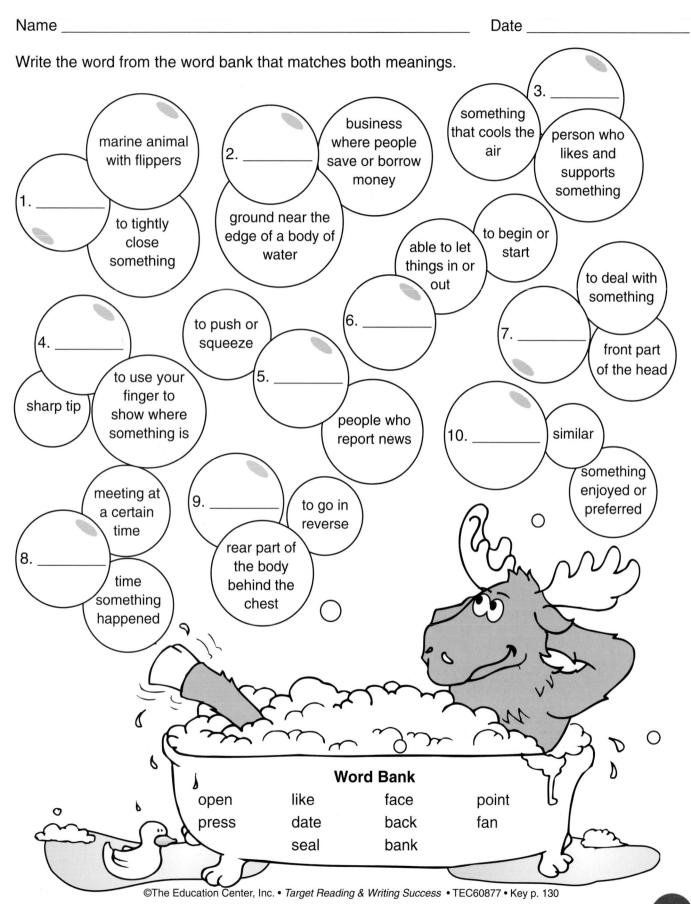

1. _____
- marine animal with flippers
- to tightly close something

2. _____
- business where people save or borrow money
- ground near the edge of a body of water

3. _____
- something that cools the air
- person who likes and supports something

4. _____
- sharp tip
- to use your finger to show where something is

5. _____
- to push or squeeze
- people who report news

6. _____
- able to let things in or out
- to begin or start

7. _____
- to deal with something
- front part of the head

8. _____
- meeting at a certain time
- time something happened

9. _____
- to go in reverse
- rear part of the body behind the chest

10. _____
- similar
- something enjoyed or preferred

Word Bank

open	like	face	point
press	date	back	fan
seal		bank	

"Bee-utiful!"

Name _____ Date _____

Circle the correct meaning of the underlined word.

1. The flowers are as sweet as <u>jam</u>.

   Z. a food made from cooking fruit
   R. to press something into a small space

2. There are too many flowers to <u>count</u>.

   D. to name in order
   M. a nobleman

3. Yesterday was <u>fair</u>, but I think it will rain today.

   S. pleasant
   L. a market

4. Betty <u>left</u> to go to the flower shop.

   Q. opposite of right
   Z. went away

5. I want to <u>stick</u> around and enjoy these flowers.

   C. a twig or a branch
   G. to remain or stay

6. The gardener is trying to lure us into a <u>net</u>!

   R. an object that catches something
   M. the profit left after expenses

7. Did you hear a bell <u>ring</u>?

   S. a square area used in boxing
   B. to make a clear sound

8. That means the <u>pet</u> cat is nearby.

   B. to stroke or pat
   U. a tame animal kept as a favorite

9. It is <u>rare</u> for him to enter the garden.

   E. not completely cooked
   H. not happening often

10. Now I am the <u>sole</u> bee in this garden.

   A. only
   R. the bottom of the foot

What kind of birds do bees like best?

To answer the riddle, match the circled letters to the numbered lines below.

___ ___ ___ ___ ___ ___ ___ ___
 7   8   4   1 10 6   2   3

Weary Wolf

Name _____ Date _____

Complete each sentence using the same word in each blank.
Cross off each word after using it.

1. What do people _____ when they say I am a _____ wolf?

2. Don't they know that I am the _____ of wolf that does _____ things?

3. I'll raise my _____ hand to say that I always try to do the _____ thing!

4. When I _____ a bad wolf coming, I lead my friends to a safe _____ to hide.

5. But people either _____ when they see me or shout that they want my _____.

6. People watch me every _____ and won't give me a _____ chance.

7. I wish I could use a _____ to leave a note at the pigs' _____.

8. I would tell them the real _____ of how their one-_____ house was wrecked.

9. I didn't _____ down that house; the _____ came from a falling tree.

10. If I could _____, I would write a magic _____ so people would believe me!

©The Education Center, Inc. • *Target Reading & Writing Success* • TEC60877 • Key p. 130

Well-Rested Rooster

Name _____ Date _____

Study the meaning of the underlined word.
Circle the sentence that uses the same meaning of the word.

1. Rooster has made a <u>grave</u> mistake!
   a. The boy buried his fish in a grave.
   b. The victim was in grave condition.

2. His morning <u>crow</u> usually happens at the same time each day.
   a. We heard the rooster crow.
   b. The crow flew through the air.

3. But today he slept too <u>long</u>.
   a. I long to live in the city.
   b. Will Matt take very long in the shower?

4. The <u>yard</u> is still quiet.
   a. Please cut a yard of fabric.
   b. The children play in the yard.

5. Everyone <u>will</u> be late for work.
   a. The lawyer read the will today.
   b. There will be a storm this afternoon.

6. The cows will have to <u>hold</u> their milk a little longer.
   a. I tried to hold my breath.
   b. Is the table strong enough to hold those books?

7. I hope this is not like the <u>last</u> time!
   a. I went to the store last week.
   b. How long does cheese last?

8. Farmer Frank was very <u>firm</u> with Rooster.
   a. My brother opened his own law firm.
   b. My mom is very firm about the rules.

9. He said Rooster's job wasn't <u>stable</u>, and he might lose it.
   a. The damaged building is not stable.
   b. The animals are sleeping in the stable.

10. I hope Rooster listened <u>well</u>!
    a. He did well on his test.
    b. I threw a penny in the wishing well.

Starfish Supervision

Name _____ Date _____

Color the letter of the word that completes both sentences.

1. The pole ___ is a track-and-field event.
   Sergeant Starfish guards the ___.

   (M) safe   (O) event   (S) vault

2. The ___ cashes checks daily.
   Someone found coins on the ___ of the river.

   (I) bank   (W) store   (M) place

3. The fish like to ____ out for lunch.
   The sergeant placed his files in ____.

   (L) get   (U) order   (B) boxes

4. The guard uses a ___ to measure.
   King Jellyfish is the ___ of our kingdom.

   (N) leader   (A) ruler   (D) yardstick

5. He keeps his treasure in a ____.
   The king wears medals on his ____.

   (D) vault   (O) bank   (V) chest

6. Listen to the ____ of that fish's drum.
   We ___ his team in the baseball game.

   (Y) rhythm   (M) defeated   (U) beat

7. The security customer paid his _____.
   The seagull held the fish in his _____.

   (G) beak   (H) guard   (T) bill

8. The rough water became _____.
   I was _____ waiting an hour later.

   (I) silent   (S) scared   (F) still

9. Did I _____ the shrimp dinner?
   I really _____ my best friend.

   (J) lose   (R) miss   (E) change

10. What is the _____ with the alarm?
    It doesn't ____ to him where we eat.

    (P) care   (W) trouble   (E) matter

What is the name of Sergeant Starfish's security company?

To answer the question, match the colored letters to the numbered lines below.

___ ___ ___ ___ - ___ ___ ___ ___
 8   2   5   10   1   7   4   9

Security, Inc.

Sweet Treats

Name _____ Date _____

Color the candy beside the correct meaning of the underlined word.

1. Otis sells <u>hard</u> candy in his candy store.
   - (a) very firm
   - (b) difficult

2. He puts the candy on a colored <u>plate</u>.
   - (a) a dish food is served on
   - (b) the area near which a batter stands on a baseball field

3. You can pay for the candy with a <u>check</u>.
   - (a) to see whether something is right
   - (b) a written order to a bank to pay a certain amount of money

4. He sells more candy in the <u>fall</u>.
   - (a) the season after summer
   - (b) to drop

5. Otis is saving his profits for a <u>trip</u>.
   - (a) to stumble over something and fall
   - (b) a journey

Use the uncolored meanings above to write sentences with the underlined words.

6 _____

_____

7 _____

_____

8 _____

_____

9 _____

_____

10 _____

_____

Baseball Bats?

Name _____   Date _____

Use the same word in both blanks to complete each sentence.
Cross off the word in the word bank after using it.

1. It is not _____ that the game is on the same night as the county _____.

2. The _____ where the field is charges you to _____ your car.

3. I was the only _____ who brought a _____ to keep cool.

4. The coach took a _____ full of baseballs from the _____ of his car.

5. He put on his baseball _____ and removed the _____ from his water bottle.

6. As the player got up to _____, a small _____ flew over his head.

7. The pitch was called a _____ as the player took a _____ at the ball.

8. The next batter looked at his _____ and did not _____ the pitch.

9. He started to _____ when he heard the umpire _____, "You're out!"

10. I went _____ to get snacks after the third _____ was called.

11. That woman always _____ on the walkway in front of the _____!

12. The catcher handed the _____ a large _____ of water.

13. Sweat started to _____ down his face as the other team scored a _____.

14. We saw the ball _____ on the area of _____ behind the fence.

15. Since he is the _____ of the game, he gets to pin a _____ on his hat.

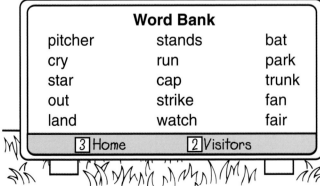

Word Bank

pitcher	stands	bat
cry	run	park
star	cap	trunk
out	strike	fan
land	watch	fair

3 Home   2 Visitors

Stocking Up!

Name _____ Date _____

Study the underlined word.
Write the letter of its definition on the matching can.

Did you unpack a <u>case</u> of books?

The lawyer took her <u>case</u>.
A. problem to be decided by law
B. container used to hold things

<u>Part</u> of the order was not delivered.

She played the lead <u>part</u>.
C. not the whole thing
D. role in a movie or play

I wanted to <u>rest</u> after the game.

The <u>rest</u> of the food will arrive Monday.
E. the part that is left over
F. to relax

Could you show me your fish <u>tank</u>?

I saw an army <u>tank</u> parked outside.
G. large container
H. vehicle used in battle

He belongs to a <u>club</u> for boys.

I forgot my favorite golf <u>club</u>.
I. group of people who hold meetings
J. stick used to hit a ball

I like to <u>dip</u> strawberries in chocolate.

Have you tried my new cheese <u>dip</u>?
K. to put into a liquid and pull out
L. sauce eaten on vegetables or chips

The new movie is a <u>hit</u>!

I <u>hit</u> the ball into the outfield.
M. to strike with a bat or racket
N. something that is popular

The fish was covered with tiny <u>scales</u>.

He weighed himself on two different <u>scales</u>.
O. small plates that cover some animals' bodies
P. instrument used to measure weight

I lost my car <u>key</u>.

The <u>key</u> to good grades is hard work.
Q. way of getting something
R. piece of metal used to open a lock

©The Education Center, Inc. • *Target Reading & Writing Success* • TEC60877 • Key p. 130

Structural Analysis
Table of Contents

Parent Communication and Student Checkups

See pages 110–115 for corresponding parent communications and student checkups (mini tests) for suffixes, prefixes, and base words.

Signed, Sealed, and Delivered?

Name _____ Date _____

Form a new word by adding **-ed** to each base word.
Color by the code.

1. carry
   _____

2. pad
   _____

3. decide
   _____

4. wait
   _____

5. hurry
   _____

6. create
   _____

7. mail
   _____

8. drop
   _____

9. seal
   _____

10. dry
    _____

11. like
    _____

12. rely
    _____

13. tape
    _____

14. slip
    _____

15. jot
    _____

16. study
    _____

Color Code
base word stayed the same = red
final **e** was dropped = yellow
final consonant was doubled = green
y was changed to **i** = blue

Bumbling Bog Band

Color the correct **-ing** form of the word to reveal
the path to the missing guitar.

	in the sand	behind a log	on a boat	in the guitar case
1. sing	singeing	singging	sinning	singing
2. tune	tunying	tuneing	tuning	tunning
3. strum	struming	strumeing	strumming	strummng
4. croak	croakking	croaking	crocking	croking
5. click	clicing	clikking	clicking	clickeing
6. arrive	arriveing	arriving	arrivig	arrivving
7. tap	tapping	tapeing	taping	tapinng
8. drum	druming	drumming	drumeing	drumying
9. hurry	hurring	hurrying	hurying	hurryng
10. call	calling	caling	callying	calleing
11. buzz	buzing	buzzing	buzzying	buzzig
12. take	tacking	takeing	taking	takking
13. swim	swimying	swiming	swimmng	swimming
14. play	playeing	playying	plaing	playing
15. slither	slithing	slitherring	slithering	slitherng
16. share	sharring	sharing	shareing	sharinng
17. float	floating	floatying	floatting	floatingg
18. celebrate	celebrateing	celebrating	celebratting	celebratng
19. fret	frettig	freting	fretting	freteing
20. satisfy	satisfing	satisfying	sattisfying	satisffying

Dig In!

Name _____ Date _____

Write each base word on the lines.

1. growing

2. watered

3. planned

4. fertilizing

5. raked

6. added

7. breathed

8. snipped

9. climbing

10. hoeing

11. beginning

12. prepared

13. transplanted

14. dropping

15. living

16. placed

Why did Flo bury her money in her garden?

To find out, write the circled letters in order on the lines below.

Because she _____ _____ _____ _____ _____ _____ _____ _____ _____ _____ _____ _____ _____ _____ _____ _____ .

Super Spinners

Name _____   Date _____

Form a new word by adding the suffix to a word from the web's center.
Cross off each word after using it.
The first one has been done for you.

-ness
likeness

-ness
_____

-ness
_____

-ness
_____

-ness:
quality of

-able
_____

-able
_____

~~like~~	polite
care	dispose
help	penny
kind	spot
price	happy
enjoy	accept
wash	end
weak	thick

-ness
_____

-ness
_____

-able
_____

-able
_____

-less
_____

-less
_____

-less:
without

-less
_____

-less
_____

-able:
able to

-less
_____

-less
_____

Suffixes: *-able, -less, -ness*

The Icing on the Cake

Name _____   Date _____

Use a suffix listed below to write a word that matches each definition.
The number in parentheses tells how many times to use that suffix.

-ly
in the
manner of
(6)

-er
one
who does
(4)

-ful
full of
(4)

1. in a proud manner   _____
2. one who bakes   _____
3. full of delight   _____
4. one who sells groceries   _____
5. in a loud way   _____

6. in a smooth manner   _____
7. full of cheer   _____
8. in a happy way   _____
9. one who teaches   _____

10. full of skill   _____
11. one who cleans   _____
12. in a hungry manner   _____
13. full of beauty   _____
14. in a neat way   _____

Mermaid Princess

Name _____ Date _____

Add the suffix **-ist** or **-tion** to form a new word.
Write the meaning of the new word.
The first one has been done for you.

> **-ist:** one who practices
> **-tion:** the act of

1. conserve + ⟨tion⟩ = _conservation_____
   _the act of conserving_____

2. organize + ☐ = _____
   _____

3. biology + ☐ = _____
   _____

4. locate + ☐ = _____
   _____

5. tour + ☐ = _____
   _____

6. ecology + ☐ = _____
   _____

7. protect + ☐ = _____
   _____

8. science + ☐ = _____
   _____

9. communicate + ☐ = _____
   _____

10. art + ☐ = _____
    _____

Suffixes: *-ist, -tion*

View From the Top

Name _____ Date _____

Use the word bank to fill in the blanks.
Cross off each word after using it.

Gail and Gary are climbing Old Mount Baldy. Gail has practiced

climbing for four weeks. So she feels _____ that

she can keep up with Gary. He is two years older and more

_____ than Gail. Gail had felt _____

before she started practicing. But now Gail is sure she can keep up.

Gary and Gail are _____ as they climb the peak.

If they are _____, they might stumble. Falling would

be very _____.

Gail's new water bottle leaks. "It's _____!" she

cries. "It would be _____ if I had a water bottle that

actually held water." Gary laughs and hands Gail his

old beat-up canteen.

While Gail drinks Gary's water, Gary looks

around at the _____ horizon.

Gary announces, "We did it! We are at

the top!"

"And look," Gail says, "Now I know

why it's called Old Mount Baldy. It's

completely _____!"

Word Bank
helpful
hopeful
powerful
careful
endless
useless
painful
hopeless
treeless
careless

Bone "Re-search"

Name _____ Date _____

Use *non-*, *re-*, or *pre-* to form a word that matches each definition.
The first one has been done for you.

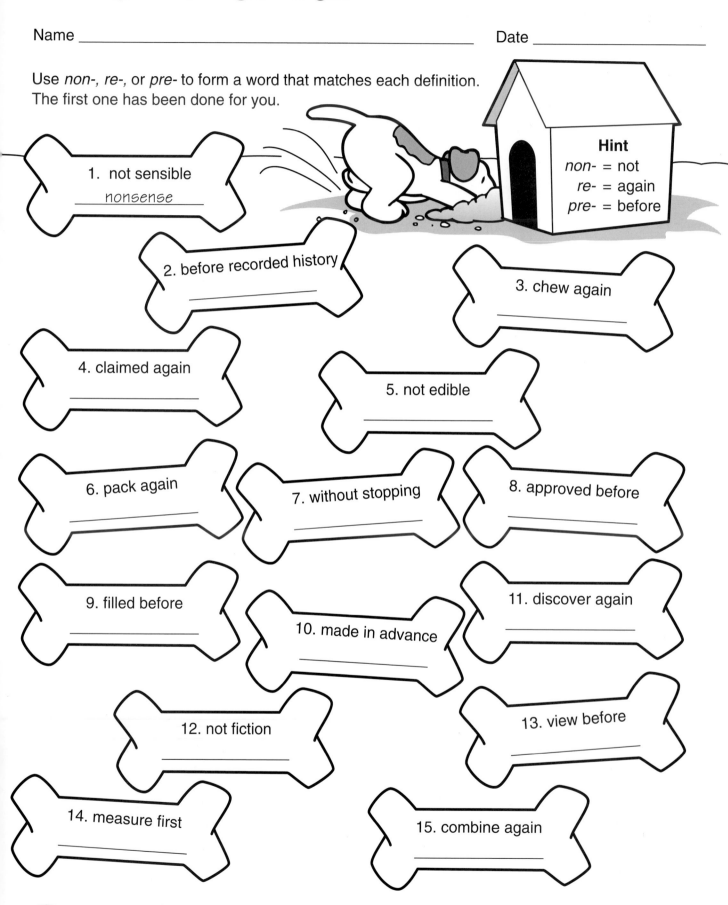

Hint
non- = not
re- = again
pre- = before

1. not sensible
   nonsense

2. before recorded history
   _____

3. chew again
   _____

4. claimed again
   _____

5. not edible
   _____

6. pack again
   _____

7. without stopping
   _____

8. approved before
   _____

9. filled before
   _____

10. made in advance
    _____

11. discover again
    _____

12. not fiction
    _____

13. view before
    _____

14. measure first
    _____

15. combine again
    _____

Prefixes: non-, re-, pre-

Super Sleuth

Name _____   Date _____

Match each word to its meaning.

_____ 1. disappear
_____ 2. disbelieve
_____ 3. subset
_____ 4. disorder
_____ 5. subconscious
_____ 6. disinterested
_____ 7. displaced
_____ 8. substandard
_____ 9. substructure
_____ 10. disobey
_____ 11. submarine
_____ 12. disagree
_____ 13. discover
_____ 14. subsoil

within or under another set
E

not interested
P

to make known or uncover
T

an under structure
S

to no longer be seen
L

below standard
K

not having order
N

to not agree
D

soil that is under the surface
I

below consciousness
M

not in place
C

to not believe
A

a ship that travels underwater
U

to not obey
R

What kind of shoes did the detective wear?

To solve the riddle, match the letters above to the numbered lines below.

_____ _____ _____ _____ _____ _____ _____ _____
  9   4   3   2   8   3   10   9

A Perfect Landing?

Name _____ Date _____

Color the word that matches each definition to show the path to Henrietta's landing spot.

Hint:
uni- = one
bi- = two
tri- = three

1. a three-sided shape	triangle	rectangle	square
2. has one wheel and pedals	bicycle	unicycle	tricycle
3. relating to two states	nation	bisect	bistate
4. a stand that has three legs	brace	trilogy	tripod
5. glasses lens that has two parts	unify	bifocal	bivalve
6. an imaginary animal with one horn	unicorn	uniform	zephyr
7. takes place every three weeks	triweekly	trilogy	trio
8. made up of three	tricky	triple	tribute
9. has two levels	uni-level	bi-level	tri-level
10. a group of three	triumph	tribute	trio
11. using one language	English	unilingual	bilingual
12. takes place every two months	binocular	bimonthly	semiannual
13. a dinosaur with three horns	triceratops	brontosaur	stegosaurus
14. tooth with two points	molar	bicuspid	premolar
15. having three colors	colorful	tricolor	triplicate

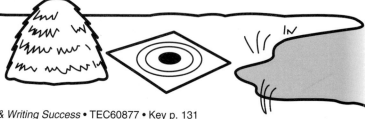

Prefixes: *uni-, bi-, tri-*

Nothin' to It!

Use the prefix *im-*, *in-*, or *un-* to form a new word that means the opposite of each clue.
Color each ball after using its prefix.

in- in- in- un- im- un- in- im- un- un- im- in- in- im- un- im-

The prefixes *im-*, *in-*,
and *un-* all mean "not."

1. known
_____

2. clear
_____

3. active
_____

4. measurable
_____

5. touched
_____

6. sure
_____

7. dependent
_____

8. edible
_____

9. even
_____

10. perfect
_____

11. destructible
_____

12. lock
_____

13. patient
_____

14. polite
_____

15. expensive
_____

16. complete
_____

Safe!

Name _____ Date _____

Write each word's base on the line.
The first one has been done for you.

renewable

$\dfrac{n}{1}$ $\dfrac{e}{2}$ $\dfrac{w}{3}$

inaction

___ ___ ___
4   5   6

unreadable

___ ___ ___ ___
7   8   9   10

disrespectful

___ ___ ___ ___ ___ ___ ___
11 12 13 14 15 16 17

nonbreakable

___ ___ ___ ___ ___
18 19 20 21 22

unhappiness

___ ___ ___ ___ ___
23 24 25 26 27

dissatisfaction

___ ___ ___ ___ ___ ___ ___
28 29 30 31 32 33 34

unreasonable

___ ___ ___ ___ ___ ___
35 36 37 38 39 40

indigestion

___ ___ ___ ___ ___ ___
41 42 43 44 45 46

repayable

___ ___ ___
47 48 49

displacement

___ ___ ___ ___ ___
50 51 52 53 54

immigration

___ ___ ___ ___ ___ ___ ___
55 56 57 58 59 60 61

Why are police officers at the baseball game?

To solve the riddle, match the letters above to the numbered lines below.

___ ___ ___ ___   ___ ___ ___ ___ ___   ___ ___ ___ E ___ ___ ___   W ___ ___
6 23 8 34   23 15 48 19 41   28 39 55 2 39 40 61   3 52 45

___ ___ ___ ___ N ___ ___ ___   ___ ___ ___ ___ ___!
32 17 54 21 51 42 1 57   18 4 13 20 38

©The Education Center, Inc. • *Target Reading & Writing Success* • TEC60877 • Key p. 132

Whales' Tails!

Name _____   Date _____

Write each word's prefix, base, and suffix
  on the lines.
Then write the meaning of the word.
The first one has been started for you.

1. nonparticipation

non + _participate_ + _ion_

_____

_____

_____

2. unbreakable

_____ + _____ + _____

_____

_____

_____

3. pretreatment

_____ + _____ + _____

_____

_____

_____

4. uncomfortable

_____ + _____ + _____

_____

_____

_____

5. unbelievable

_____ + _____ + _____

_____

_____

_____

Hint:
un- = not
non- = not
pre- = before
-able = able to
-ment = act, result, state
-ion = act, condition

6. prearrangement

_____ + _____ + _____

_____

_____

_____

7. nonpayment

_____ + _____ + _____

_____

_____

_____

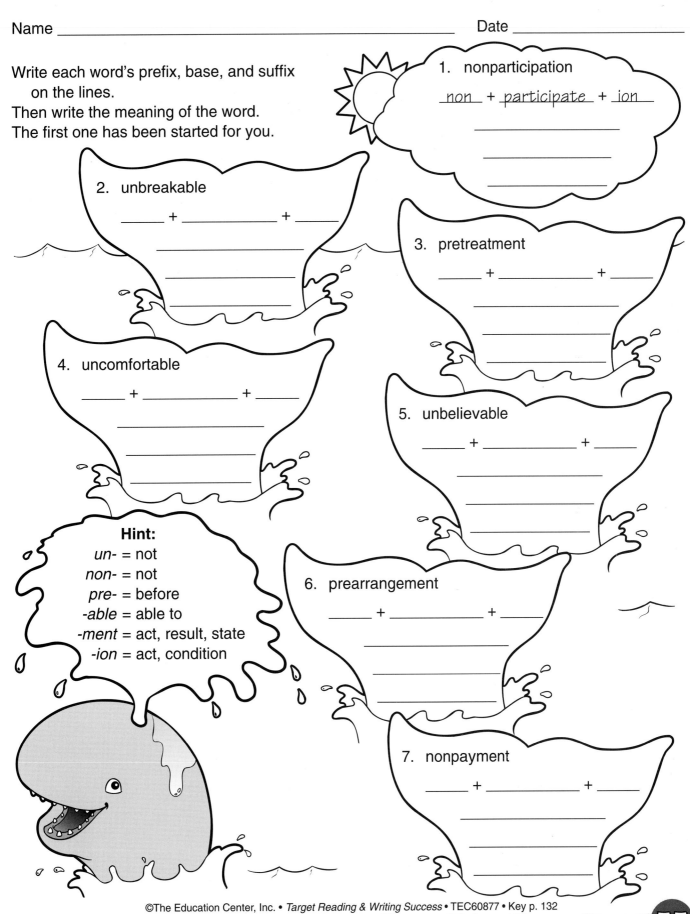

Supersize!

Name _____ Date _____

Use the prefixes, the suffixes, or both with each base
   word to make as many new words as you can.
The first one has been started for you.

It's
unbelievable!

Prefixes		Suffixes	
un-	pre-	-ful	-ness
dis-	non-	-able	-ment
re-		-ly	-less

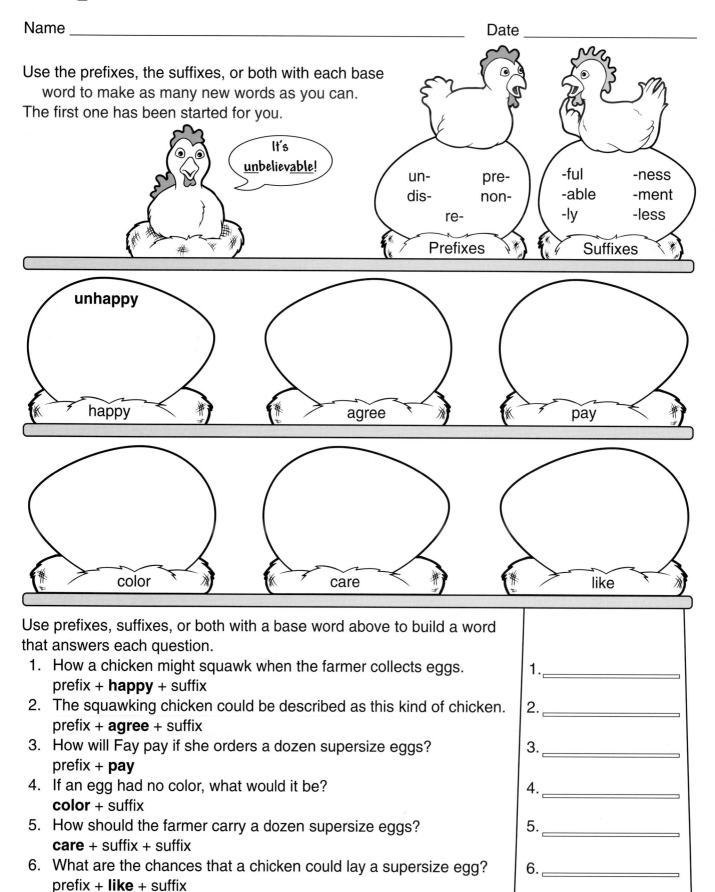

unhappy

happy

agree

pay

color

care

like

Use prefixes, suffixes, or both with a base word above to build a word
that answers each question.

1. How a chicken might squawk when the farmer collects eggs.
   prefix + **happy** + suffix
2. The squawking chicken could be described as this kind of chicken.
   prefix + **agree** + suffix
3. How will Fay pay if she orders a dozen supersize eggs?
   prefix + **pay**
4. If an egg had no color, what would it be?
   color + suffix
5. How should the farmer carry a dozen supersize eggs?
   care + suffix + suffix
6. What are the chances that a chicken could lay a supersize egg?
   prefix + **like** + suffix

1. _____
2. _____
3. _____
4. _____
5. _____
6. _____

©The Education Center, Inc. • *Target Reading & Writing Success* • TEC60877 • Key p. 132

Word Roots

Word Roots
Table of Contents

Parent Communication and Student Checkups

See pages 116–119 for corresponding parent communications and student checkups (mini tests) for word roots.

One Mixed-Up Painter

Name _____ Date _____

Underline the Greek root in each word in the word bank.
Match each meaning on a paint can to a word from the word bank.

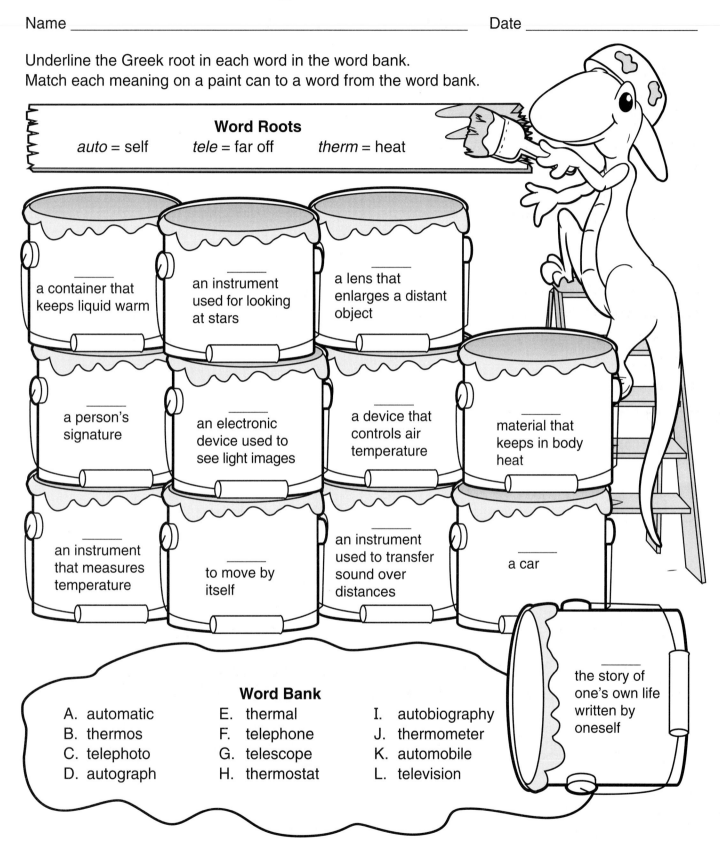

Word Roots

auto = self   *tele* = far off   *therm* = heat

_____
a container that keeps liquid warm

_____
an instrument used for looking at stars

_____
a lens that enlarges a distant object

_____
a person's signature

_____
an electronic device used to see light images

_____
a device that controls air temperature

_____
material that keeps in body heat

_____
an instrument that measures temperature

_____
to move by itself

_____
an instrument used to transfer sound over distances

_____
a car

_____
the story of one's own life written by oneself

Word Bank

A. automatic
B. thermos
C. telephoto
D. autograph

E. thermal
F. telephone
G. telescope
H. thermostat

I. autobiography
J. thermometer
K. automobile
L. television

Greek roots: *auto, tele, therm*

Mixed-Up Music

Name _____ Date _____

Circle one of the following word roots found in each word
   in a music note: *chron, cycl, graph,* or *phon.*
Fill in the blanks with words from the music notes.
Use the underlined clues to help you.

Tonight's _____ **Performance**

A. _____ Rhumba: A tale of <u>using</u>
    <u>things more than</u> once, told through song

B. Billy's _____ Ballad: The story of
    <u>Billy's life</u> set to music

C. _____ Boogie: A catchy tune
    about getting around on <u>two-wheels</u>

D. Tempos by the _____: Music
    <u>written</u> in Morse code

E. _____ Shuffle: Each
    instrument sounding at the <u>same time</u>

F. _____ Tango: Beautiful
    <u>ring tones</u> together

G. _____ Solo: A song about
    <u>circular, spinning windstorms</u>

H. Conga _____: A <u>timeline</u> of
    dance and rhythm

Many thanks to

- Phil, our _____,
  for <u>taking</u> <u>pictures</u> of the event.

- Carmen, for <u>writing</u> the program in
  _____.

Word Roots
chron = time
cycl = circle
graph = writing
phon = sound

Telephone

Chronology

calligraphy

Bicycle

Recycle

Telegraph

photographer

Synchronized

Biography

Symphony

Cyclone

Greek roots: *chron, cycl, graph, phon*

Keeping Dry

Name _____   Date _____

Group the words according to their common word roots.
Write each group of words on a toadstool.
Write what the word root means in the matching speech bubble.

photosynthesis

astrology

hydrant

asterisk

hydroplane

astronaut

telephoto

photograph

hydrate

hydroelectric

photocell

astronomy

asteriod

photocopier

hydraulic

Word root:

_____

Word root:

_____

Word root:

_____

Meaning:

Meaning:

Meaning:

Greek roots: *astr, photo, hydr*

Special Deliveries

Name _____   Date _____

Read the meanings of three common word roots on the mailbox flags.
Group the words from the envelopes according to these word roots.
Write each word on the correct mailbox.

chief or ruler

root

life

root

earth

root

geography

biology

architect

geocentric

antibiotic

patriarch

biography

geode

geothermal

biopsy

symbiotic

biome

archangel

anarchy

geology

hierarchy

monarch

geometry

Mail

©The Education Center, Inc. • *Target Reading & Writing Success* • TEC60877 • Key p. 132

Greek roots: *arch, geo, bio*

Magic on Ice?

Name _____ Date _____

Underline the word root in each boldfaced word.
Use the meaning of the word root to help you answer the question.
Circle the letter under the yes or no column.

Word Roots
micro = small
mono = one
mech = machine

		Yes	No
1.	Would a **mechanic** sew a torn hockey jersey?	S	A
2.	Can the coach's pregame speech to his players be called a **monologue?**	C	T
3.	Would you use a **micrometer** to measure a large parking lot?	E	D
4.	Could an ice machine have **mechanical** trouble?	T	C
5.	Would you need a **microscope** to see a hockey rink?	I	S
6.	Could a magician keep his schedule in a **microcomputer?**	O	L
7.	Would you describe a magician's rainbow-colored coat as **monochromatic?**	S	T
8.	Would a **microphone** help the announcer during the game?	R	A
9.	Would you compare a very long hockey game to a **microwave?**	V	I
10.	Could you see the score if the scoreboard's **mechanism** breaks?	O	H

What do a hockey player and a magician have in common?
To solve the riddle, match the circled letters to the numbered lines below.

Both ____ ____ ____ ____ ____ ____ ____ ____ ____ __K__ ____ !
       3   6   10   1   7   4   8   9   2   5

Greetings From Planet Primate

Name _____ Date _____

Match each boldfaced word to its definition on a rock.
Use context clues and the meanings of the word roots to help you.

Word Roots
gram = thing written
meter = measure
scope = view
sphere = ball, sphere

Telegram from Astronaut Chimp N. Zee

I have arrived safely on Planet Primate. It didn't take long for my ship to break through the planet's **atmosphere.** The **telescope** worked nicely. I could see Earth clearly from here. I have measured the **perimeter** of my landing zone. My computer **program** calculated how far I walked as I searched for artifacts. I found tiny rocks in the planet's southern **hemisphere.** I used the **microscope** to look at them. Each rock was in the shape of a **sphere.** One even had a **diagram** of a **kaleidoscope.** It had several drawings showing how it works. I have concluded that the beings on this planet have **grammar** and math skills. I will be returning soon.

instrument
for viewing bits
of colored objects
_____

the air
surrounding
a planet
_____

instructions that
a computer follows
_____

half of a
globe or sphere
_____

instrument
for viewing very
small objects
_____

round body
like a ball
_____

rules for
speaking and
writing
_____

instrument
for viewing
distant objects
_____

a sketch or
drawing that
explains how
something works
_____

the distance
around an area
_____

©The Education Center, Inc. • *Target Reading & Writing Success* • TEC60877 • Key p. 132
Greek roots: *gram, meter, scope, sphere*

Colorful Crossword

Name _____   Date _____

Underline one of the following roots for each word on a crayon: *rupt, scrib,* or *script.*
Use the words to complete the puzzle.
Color each crayon after you use the word.

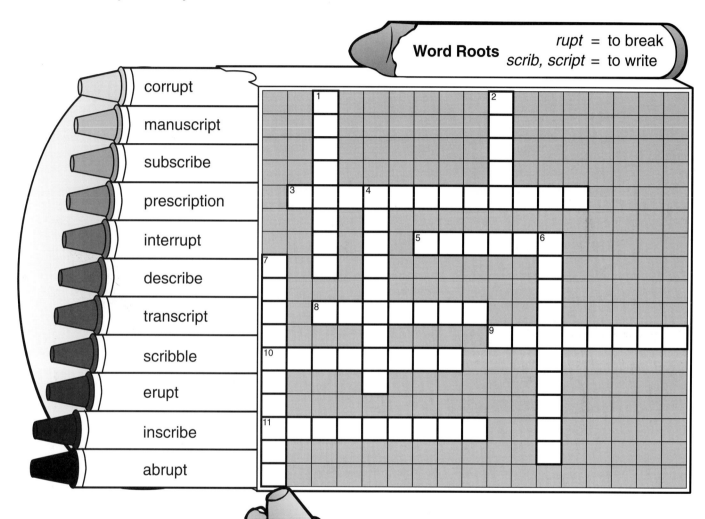

Word Roots
rupt = to break
scrib, script = to write

corrupt
manuscript
subscribe
prescription
interrupt
describe
transcript
scribble
erupt
inscribe
abrupt

Across
3. what a doctor writes to order medicine
5. happening suddenly
8. ruin or spoil
9. tell or write about something's details
10. write without being careful
11. cut in on a discussion

Down
1. write or mark on a surface
2. burst out
4. sign up to get something for a period of time
6. official typed or printed copy of something
7. written by hand

"Moose-ic" With a Beat!

Name _____ Date _____

Underline one of the following roots for each word in the word bank: *man, pop,* or *multi.*
Write each word on the matching drum.

multi = many

man = hand

pop = people

Word Bank

maneuver	manager
popular	manufactured
manual	manicure
multiply	multiple
population	popularity
multimedia	manipulate
populate	unpopular
multitude	multicolor

Play Ball!

Name _____ Date _____

Underline one of the following roots in each boldfaced word: *aud* or *ped.*
Use the meaning of these word roots to help you answer yes or no to each statement.
Color the football under the correct column.

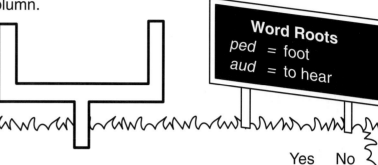

Word Roots
ped = foot
aud = to hear

	Yes	No
1. A **centipede** might use its 200 arms to catch a football.	A	L
2. Coach could give his speech in the **auditorium.**	N	C
3. Coach might use his feet if the team's **moped** runs out of gas.	A	T
4. The coach might listen to a singer's **audition** before she could sing at halftime.	L	D
5. Coach's **audible** shouts could be very loud.	T	S
6. Coach would get his fingernails clipped if he got a **pedicure.**	E	S
7. The coach could **pedal** his bike to practice.	F	G
8. The best way for Coach to teach **auditory** codes would be to write them.	M	F
9. The players could see their mistakes on an **audiotape** of the game.	K	E
10. The quarterback could wear a **pedometer** to see how far he can throw.	O	A

Why did the football stadium get so hot?
To solve the riddle, match the colored letters to the numbered lines below.

Because the $\overline{}_{8}\ \overline{}_{10}\ \overline{}_{2}\ \overline{}_{6}$

$\overline{}_{3}\ \overline{L}_{4}\ \overline{}_{1}\ \overline{}_{9}\ \overline{}_{7}\ \overline{}_{5}$

Dairy Farm Diary

Name _____ Date _____

Read the diary entries with mixed-up words.
Write each word on the numbered line that makes the sentence correct.

Word Roots
tract = to drag
spect = to look
port = to carry

Dear Diary,

The farm (1) **tracks** was hard to start today. I got it going and drove it out to (2) **distracted** the potatoes from the garden. I saw the goats crossing my (3) **tractor** and heading into the garden. I (4) **trace** them by jumping up and down. I was happy when they left the garden without a (5) **extract.**

1. _____
2. _____
3. _____
4. _____
5. _____

Dear Diary,

I can't wait for the goat-milking contest! This is my favorite (6) **portable.** I've got my (7) **reporter** stool and bucket ready to go. I won last year because I had a lot of (8) **sport** from my family! A (9) **transported** said that we will be (10) **support** to the contest for free.

6. _____
7. _____
8. _____
9. _____
10. _____

Dear Diary,

I heard a loud noise coming from the barn. I (11) **inspect** that something was wrong with the goats. I grabbed my (12) **expected** and went to (13) **suspected** the barn. I (14) **spectacles** to find a disaster. All I found was a goat who didn't want to be milked.

11. _____
12. _____
13. _____
14. _____

Pig Paradise

Name _____ Date _____

If the words in a mud puddle have the same meaning, color the puddle.

Use what you know about word roots to help you decide.

Connect the colored puddles to show the path through the maze.

Word Roots
fin = end
equa = even
form = a shape

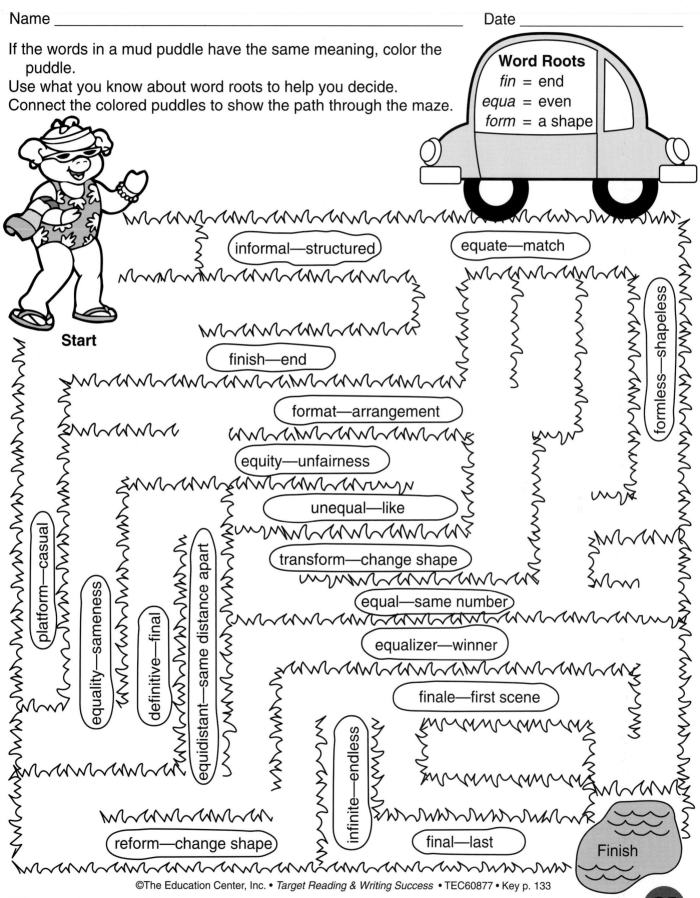

Start

informal—structured

equate—match

formless—shapeless

finish—end

format—arrangement

equity—unfairness

unequal—like

transform—change shape

equal—same number

platform—casual

equality—sameness

definitive—final

equidistant—same distance apart

equalizer—winner

finale—first scene

infinite—endless

reform—change shape

final—last

Finish

Latin roots: *fin, equa, form*

Oops!

Name _____   Date _____

Find the root for each word.
Color by the code.

Color Code
mob = yellow
min = brown
dict = orange

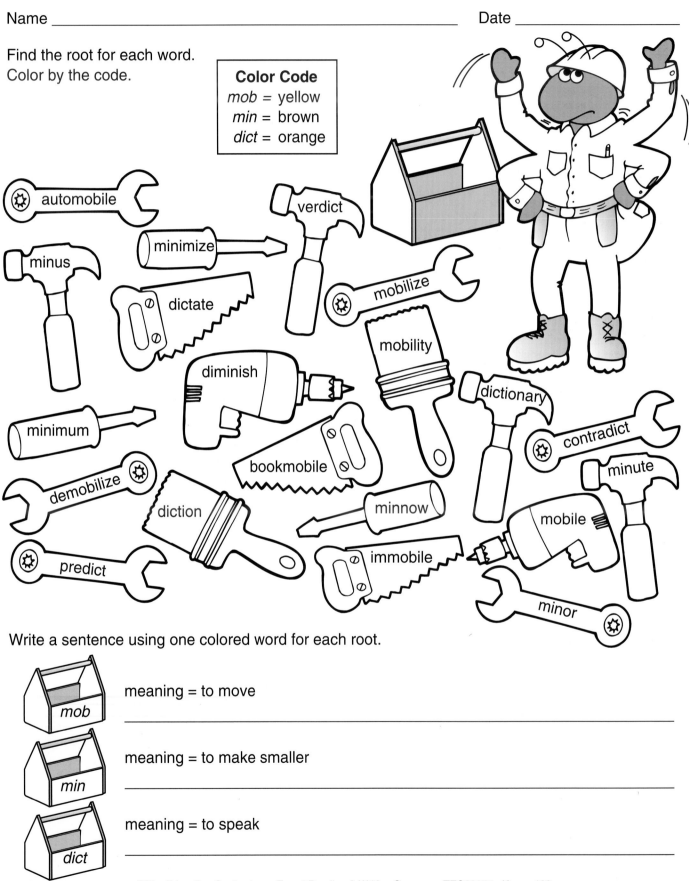

automobile
verdict
minimize
minus
mobilize
dictate
diminish
mobility
dictionary
minimum
contradict
minute
demobilize
bookmobile
diction
minnow
mobile
immobile
predict
minor

Write a sentence using one colored word for each root.

mob — meaning = to move

_____

min — meaning = to make smaller

_____

dict — meaning = to speak

_____

Figurative Language

Figurative Language
Table of Contents

Parent Communication and Student Checkups

See pages 120–123 for corresponding parent communications and student checkups (mini tests) for the skills listed above.

Bird Talk

Name _____ Date _____

Match each underlined idiom to its meaning.

1. Betty said the new straw she's using is so stiff it's <u>for the birds</u>!

2. Bernard leaves at 6:00 A.M. because he thinks <u>the early bird catches the worm</u>.

3. Bo saw his favorite food in the feeder. He is <u>walking on air</u>!

4. Barbara's first-place finish is <u>a feather in her cap</u>!

5. Barry is getting restless. I think he's ready to <u>fly the coop</u>.

6. If Ben hears Brian's secret it's going to <u>open a can of worms</u>!

7. Betsy is <u>putting all her eggs in one basket</u> by selling her nest to open a flight school.

8. Baron is so smart, <u>the sky's the limit</u>!

9. Bill is <u>going to take him under his wing</u> and teach him how to fly.

10. Bonnie is so grouchy you have to <u>walk on eggshells around her</u>.

☐ an accomplishment or honor

☐ there is no limit on what can be achieved

☐ unimportant, not worth anything

☐ to be very happy and excited

☐ be careful with what is said or done

☐ taking a chance on a single thing or idea

☐ an early start gives a better chance of success

☐ escape or go away suddenly

☐ cause trouble

☐ help or guide someone

Track Meet

Name _____ Date _____

Match each idiom to its meaning.

1. jump the gun

    _____

2. off the beaten track

    _____

3. if the shoe fits, wear it

    _____

4. run circles around someone

    _____

5. the shoe is on the other foot

    _____

START **FINISH**

T. to do something better than another person

D. energy and enthusiasm

O. when something is the opposite from what it used to be

A. if a comment about you seems true, admit it

B. to be nervous or afraid

R. doing something at the same rate as someone else

E. not often used or not well known

W. the last part of a journey

F. to do or say something before you should

S. to start a journey

10. getting cold feet

    _____

9. hit the road

    _____

8. the last leg

    _____

7. neck and neck

    _____

6. get-up-and-go

    _____

What idiom did the coach tell his runners before the race?

To find out, match the letters to the numbered lines below.

"Put your __ __ __ __ __ __ O T   F O R __ __ __ __! "
             10 2 9 4   1 5   8 3 7 6

One Determined Rabbit

Name _____ Date _____

Underline the idiom in each sentence.

A. Rodney had butterflies in his stomach before attempting the trick.

B. He couldn't put his finger on why he was having trouble.

C. Rodney knew he could do it, but he had to keep his chin up!

D. He started to think he was wet behind the ears when it came to skating.

E. Rodney was all ears as his friend told him he just needed a new skateboard.

F. A new skateboard would cost an arm and a leg!

G. Maybe he could clean and repair his old one with some elbow grease.

H. Rodney put his foot down and decided that he was going to do the trick.

I. He said, "Keep your eyes peeled for my next trick!"

J. His friend told Rodney to break a leg!

Match the underlined idioms to the meanings below.

☐ inexperienced

☐ describe exactly

☐ a feeling of nervousness in the stomach

☐ do a great job

☐ have courage

☐ ready to listen

☐ watch carefully

☐ cost a lot of money

☐ hard work

☐ to take a firm stand

Scarlet Skunk, Superstar!

Name _____   Date _____

Use the words on the film to complete each well-known simile.

| thunder | bell | monkeys | picture | mouse |

| bee | honey | diamonds | bird | stars |

⭐ 1 Scarlet Skunk was as pretty as a _____ walking down the red carpet.

⭐ 2 The sequins on her dazzling gown sparkled like _____.

⭐ 3 Her eyes shone like _____ as her picture was taken.

⭐ 4 Her fans cheered as loud as _____ when she walked by.

⭐ 5 One fan said, "She sang like a _____ in the movie!"

⭐ 6 Before her award was announced, the crowd was as quiet as a _____.

⭐ 7 Scarlet spoke as clear as a _____ when she accepted the award.

⭐ 8 The director said that Scarlet was as sweet as _____.

⭐ 9 At the awards party, the cast and crew chattered like _____.

⭐ 10 Scarlet knew she'd be as busy as a _____ after winning the award.

Picture This!

Name _____ Date _____

Write words on each easel to complete the similes.
The first one has been done for you.

1. as quiet as
   a mouse
   falling snow

2. as rough as

3. as dark as

4. as straight as

5. as deep as

6. as tasty as

7. as tiny as

8. as hard as

9. as slow as

10. strong like

11. sparkly like

12. gentle like

Spreading the News

Name _____ Date _____

Draw a line to the matching banner piece to complete each metaphor.

The plane is a messenger in the sky.

1 | The soft, fuzzy slippers are

2 | The flowers in the meadow are

3 | The girl's blowing hair is

4 | The rain on the window is

5 | The rising moon is

6 | The stream of traffic is

7 | The frightened child was

8 | The runner is

9 | The book is

10 | The ice pop is

11 | The young boy's room is

12 | The girl's laughter is

A. a treasure chest of toys.

B. a graceful deer.

C. a welcome night-light.

D. a blanket of color.

E. a bowl of Jell-O gelatin.

F. balls of cotton on my feet.

G. a blast of arctic air.

H. a stream of tears.

I. a happy song.

J. a magic carpet flying the reader to an exciting place.

K. a flag in the wind.

L. a parade of ants.

Boasting Buckaroos

Name _____   Date _____

Complete each metaphor in the space provided.
The first one has been done for you.

1. My new horse _is a lightning_ _____ _bolt._ _____

2. My swinging lasso _____ _____

3. My worn boots _____ _____

4. My bright bandana _____ _____

5. My spicy chili _____ _____

6. My shiny spurs _____ _____

7. My new cowboy hat _____ _____

8. My red barn _____ _____

9. My warm campfire _____ _____

10. My old jeans _____ _____

11. My new saddle _____ _____

12. My strong fence _____ _____

Rim Shot

Name _____   Date _____

If the sentence uses onomatopoeia, color the
    circle in the yes column.
Underline the word that shows onomatopoeia.
If the sentence does not use onomatopoeia,
    color the ball in the no column.

		Yes	No
1.	The loud buzz sounded as the game began.	O	E
2.	Greta noisily dribbled down the court.	A	D
3.	Swish! The ball slid through the net!	B	E
4.	The fans roared for the first basket.	F	T
5.	Both teams rumbled back down the court.	C	N
6.	Glenda quietly drove in to the basket.	H	I
7.	The ball crashed into the backboard.	A	Y
8.	The crowd groaned as the ball dropped in.	P	N
9.	Tweet! The whistle blew to stop the game.	S	C
10.	"There was a foul!" yelled the referee.	H	B
11.	Glenda's shoes squeaked at the line.	G	M
12.	The crowd was silent while Glenda shot.	T	V
13.	The ball hit the rim with a clunk.	L	U
14.	Then the ball bounced to the floor.	K	W
15.	The ball's thud echoed in the gym.	J	D

Why do basketball players love cookies?

To solve the riddle, match the uncolored letters to the numbered lines below.

Because ____ ____ ____ ____   ____ ____ ____   ____ ____ ____ ____   ____ ____ ____ ____!
           4 10 1 7   9 2 5   15 13 8 14   12 6 3 11

Jukebox Jazz

Name _____ Date _____

Choose the onomatopoeic word that best matches each sound described.

①	a stone dropped in water _____	⑧	a door being slammed shut _____
②	stepping on a pile of leaves _____	⑨	sharpening a pencil _____
③	riding on a school bus _____	⑩	footsteps in the hall _____
④	drinking soda from a straw _____	⑪	typing on a computer keyboard _____
⑤	a woodpecker pecking on an old tree _____	⑫	shaking an open newspaper _____
⑥	an afternoon thunderstorm _____	⑬	popcorn cooking _____
⑦	the school's bell _____	⑭	a barking dog _____

	ping	woof	splash	
pop	thump	clomp	varoom	grind
crash	rumble	ring	rat a tat	click
grate	bang	whir	arf	plop
crunch	rustle	slurp		

It's a Jungle Out There!

Name _____   Date _____

Rewrite each set of words to form an alliterative sentence.
The first one has been done for you.

1. sundown snazzy at slither the snakes sea along six

   _____Six snazzy_____
   _____snakes slither_____
   _____along the sea_____
   _____at sundown._____

2. turtles tigers tutus two tutor in teenage ten

3. ate of playing after polo the pickles penguins piles

4. gazelle grouchy the greets guests guppy its

5. flocks fancy fluff their of flamingos feathers

6. jam the juggled sun jackrabbit July of a jars in

7. banging blue bats on their banjos were big

8. has everything elk Ed's eaten nearly

Candy Coating

Name _____ Date _____

Use the subject and verb pair on each
candy to write an alliterative sentence.
The first one has been done for you.

My, these mango mints just melt in your mouth!

1. _____
2. _____
3. _____
4. _____
5. _____
6. _____
7. _____
8. _____
9. _____
10. _____
11. _____
12. _____

- mints melt
- geese gobble
- Ben bites
- cheetah chews
- Ronnie wraps
- iguana ices
- tiger tastes
- Nora nibbles
- deer dips
- leopard licks
- Olive overhears
- ant adds

You Don't Say

Name _____ Date _____

Underline the part of each sentence that is hyperbole.
Write what you think the hyperbole means.

I flew a million miles last week!

1. Fifi's new ring is so shiny that she has to wear sunglasses to look at it.

   _____

   _____

2. My hamster eats so much that it weighs more than a hippo.

   _____

   _____

3. It is so cold outside that my fingers turned into icicles.

   _____

4. I can skip so fast that even a cheetah can't catch me.

   _____

5. My pillow is so hard I dented my head.

   _____

6. My brother's socks smell so bad even a skunk ran away.

   _____

7. The sandwich I found in my locker was so old the mold was a fossil.

   _____

8. My room is so messy that I haven't seen my bed for two weeks.

   _____

Add hyperbole to complete each sentence below.

9. The school bus was so old _____.

10. There were so many people in the swimming pool _____.

11. Oscar drank so much water he _____.

12. Madge ran so far _____.

Reference Usage

Reference Usage
Table of Contents

Parent Communication and Student Checkups

See pages 124–125 for corresponding parent communications and student checkups (mini tests) for dictionary skills.

"Mouse-terpieces"

Name _____ Date _____

Match each set of framed words to a pair of guide words.

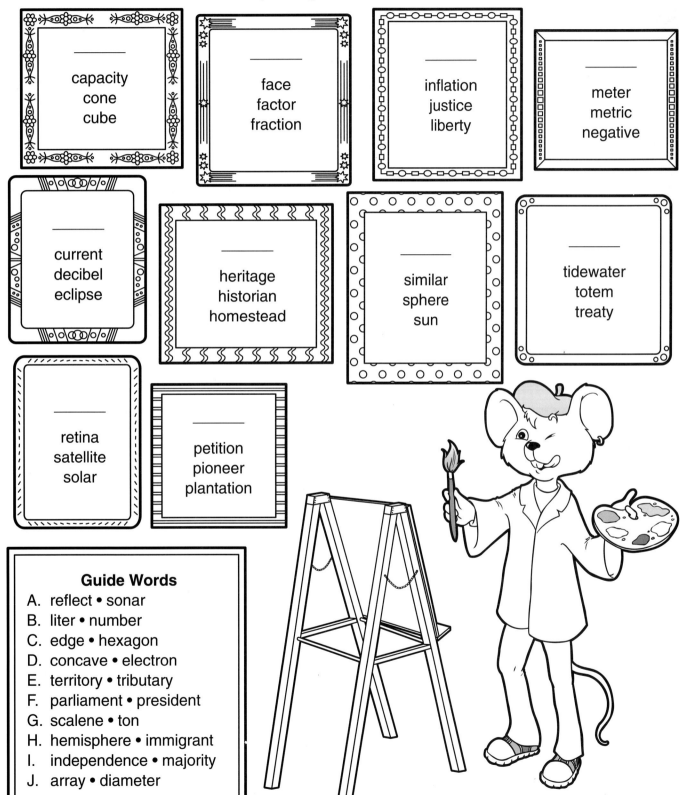

___
capacity
cone
cube

___
face
factor
fraction

___
inflation
justice
liberty

___
meter
metric
negative

___
current
decibel
eclipse

___
heritage
historian
homestead

___
similar
sphere
sun

___
tidewater
totem
treaty

___
retina
satellite
solar

___
petition
pioneer
plantation

Guide Words
A. reflect • sonar
B. liter • number
C. edge • hexagon
D. concave • electron
E. territory • tributary
F. parliament • president
G. scalene • ton
H. hemisphere • immigrant
I. independence • majority
J. array • diameter

Fact-Finding Ferrets

Name _____ Date _____

Match each item to a book and set of guide words that you would use to find the information.

Where would you find that...

1. A *degree* is a unit of measure.

2. A *nuthatch* is a small bird that looks for food in trees.

3. A *century* is a time period of 100 years.

4. A *number sequence* is a group of numbers that come one after another.

5. A *frontier* is an area that separates settled land and wilderness.

6. *Tyranny* means "harsh or unfair rule."

7. A *pentagon* is a flat shape with five sides and five angles.

8. An *equation* is a math sentence that says two things are equal.

9. A *zoologist* is a person who studies animals and how they live.

10. *Conduct* means "to carry something."

Social Studies p. 554
calvary • culture _____

Science p. 427
ultraviolet • zoom _____

Math p. 304
decagon • digit _____

Math p. 305
dimension • equilateral _____

Math p. 321
octagon • positive number _____

Science p. 425
naturalist • orangutan _____

Social Studies p. 557
fall line • fugitive _____

Science p. 421
chemical • cylinder _____

Social Studies p. 575
territory • tyrant _____

Math p. 320
negative • numeral _____

Glossary: guide words and meaning

Fashionable Flowers

Name _____ Date _____

Use the glossary to complete each sentence.

Glossary

anther (an'•thər) *noun* The part of the flower that holds pollen

egg (eg) *noun* A tiny cell that makes a new plant

fruit (froot) *noun* The part of a plant that holds the seed

ovule (äv'•yool) *noun* A tiny egg or seed

petal (pet'•əl) *noun* A colorful part of a flower

pollen (päl'•ən) *noun* The yellow powder in a flower, which fertilizes another flower

seed (sēd) *noun* The part of a plant that becomes a new plant

stamen (sta'•mən) *noun* The flower part that creates pollen

stigma (stig'•mə) *noun* The sticky tip of a flower's pistil

tube (toob) *noun* A long, narrow, hollow piece of the plant

---

1. The sticky part in the middle of a flower is called the ◯__ __ __ __ __.

2. Around the stigma are slender stems with buttons on top that hold pollen. These buttons are called __ __ __◯__ __ __.

3. Inside the anthers is a special yellow dust called ◯__ __ __ __ __.

4. Pollen is made inside the __ __ __ __◯__.

5. The stamen is usually surrounded by colorful __ __ __ __◯__.

6. Pollen from one plant lands on the stigma of the same kind of plant. When this happens, a narrow ◯__ __ __ grows.

7. The tube pushes down into the part of the plant called the __ __◯__ __.

8. The ovule is an ◯__ __.

9. The ovule becomes a ◯__ __ __ which contains a baby plant.

10. The part protecting the seed is the __◯__ __ __.

What do flowers like to wear?
To answer the riddle, write the circled letter that matches each number below.

"P ___ ___ A___ " ___ ___ ___ ___ ___ ___ ___
   8 6   5   3 7 1 2 4 10 9

A, "Bee," C

Name _____ Date _____

Write the three words that go between each pair of guide words on the hives.

1. beeswax

   behavior

beagle   before   beet
belch   beginner

2. colony

   combat

column   cocoa   comb
concert   colt

3. flower

   fly

fluff   flea   flutter
flip   flute

4. honeycomb

   horn

hoop   honk   horror
hobo   honor

5. insect

   instead

inspire   inspect   instruct
instant   inner

6. nectar

   nerve

needle   necessary   neon
navy   neighbor

7. pollen

   pony

poncho   poodle   polygon
pollute   poll

8. tip

   toboggan

title   tire   tight
toad   tiny

9. wing

   wise

wizard   wink   wiry
wicker   wisdom

Bobbing for Apples

Name _____ Date _____

Write on each barrel the guide words that best match each set of words.

1.
_____
fruity
fudge
fumble
fun
_____

2.
_____
blow
bluff
boardwalk
boast
_____

3.
_____
guarantee
guess
guild
guilty
_____

4.
_____
orchestra
organize
ornament
orphanage
_____

5.
_____
seesaw
segment
seize
seltzer
_____

6.
_____
pollute
pomp
popular
porcupine
_____

7.
_____
varnish
varsity
vegetable
veil
_____

8.
_____
hasten
hatchery
hawk
haystack
_____

9.
_____
delivery
demonstrate
denial
department
_____

10.
_____
cinch
circus
citizen
citrus
_____

haze	dependable	pork	cider
semester	fruit	orthodontics	grow
civil	pollinate	seed	funnel
harvest	guitar	blossom	orchard
variety	bobbin	delicious	velour

Proud as a Peacock?

Name _____ Date _____

Color the correct answer for each question below.

1.	Does *perennial* (pər•en′•ē•əl) have four syllables?	Yes	No
2.	Does the second syllable in *papoose* (pa•poos′) sound the same as *moose?*	Yes	No
3.	Does the first *a* in *plaza* (pla′•zə) have the same sound as the letter *a* in *ape?*	Yes	No
4.	Is the letter *e* in *procrastinate* (prō•kras′•tə•nāt) silent?	Yes	No
5.	Is the final sound in *phonograph* (fō′•nə•graf) the same as the final sound in *leaf?*	Yes	No
6.	Does the letter *y* in *pyramid* (pir′•ə•mid) have a short *i* sound?	Yes	No
7.	Does *peacock* (pē′•käk) have three syllables?	Yes	No
8.	Does the third syllable in *parallel* (per′•ə•lel) contain two *l* sounds?	Yes	No
9.	Does the letter *u* in *pupa* (pyoo′•pə) sound the same as the letter *u* in *up?*	Yes	No
10.	Does *process* (präs′•es) have two *s* sounds?	Yes	No
11.	Does the second syllable in *plateau* (pla•tō) sound the same as *show?*	Yes	No
12.	Does the second syllable in *posture* (pas′•chər) contain an *s* sound?	Yes	No
13.	Does *poncho* (pän′•chō) contain only one long *o* sound?	Yes	No
14.	Is the second syllable in *portfolio* (pôrt•fo′•lē•ō) stressed the most?	Yes	No
15.	Do *porpoise* (pôr′•pəs) and *parcel* (pär′•səl) have the same *s* sound?	Yes	No

Where does a peacock go when it loses its tail?

To solve the riddle, write the boldfaced letters from the "yes" questions in order on the lines below.

A " ___ ___ – ___ ___ ___ ___ "

___ ___ ___ ___ ___ !

Desert Detective

Name _____ Date _____

Use the dictionary entry to answer the questions below.

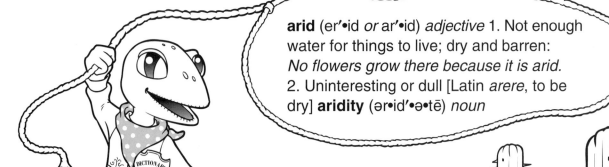

arid (er'•id *or* ar'•id) *adjective* 1. Not enough water for things to live; dry and barren: *No flowers grow there because it is arid.* 2. Uninteresting or dull [Latin *arere*, to be dry] **aridity** (ər•id'•ə•tē) *noun*

1. Draw a box around the main entry word.

2. How many syllables are in the word *arid?* _____

3. Draw a circle around the pronunciation.

4. Put an X over the part of speech.

5. Write the number of definitions *arid* has. _____

6. Draw a line under the example sentence.

7. Write the other word that is a form of the word *arid.* Tell the part of speech it is. _____

_____

8. Write the language that *arid* came from. _____

9. Write two words that have the same meaning as *arid.* _____

10. Write a sentence using the word *arid.* _____

_____

Peeping In

Name _____ Date _____

Use the sample dictionary pages to answer the questions.

Wow! It says we are small parrots!

parade (pə•rād′) *noun* 1. A march or procession in a ceremonial event or exhibition

parade (pə•rād′) *verb* 1. To march in a formation 2. To show off

paraffin (par′•ə•fin) *noun* A white, waxy substance used for sealing food or making candles and waxed paper

paragraph (par′•ə•graf) *noun* Part of a written piece, made up of one or more sentences about a single topic or idea. It begins on a new line that is usually indented

parakeet (par′•ə•kēt) *noun* A small, slender parrot with a long, pointed tail

parallel (par′•ə•lel) *adjective* 1. Moving in the same direction but never meeting and always being the same distance apart at all points 2. Alike or similar

parallel (par′•ə•lel) *noun* 1. A parallel line or surface 2. A similarity 3. Any of the imaginary lines on the earth's surface that are the same direction as the equator and which mark latitude

parallelogram (par •ə•lel′•ə•gram) *noun* A four-sided flat figure with opposite sides that are both equal in length and parallel

paralysis (pə•ral′•ə•sis) *noun* A loss of the ability for movement or feeling in a part of the body

1. Which words have more than one meaning? _____
2. How many syllables does *parallelogram* have? _____
3. Which word is both a noun and an adjective? _____
4. What does *paraffin* mean? _____
   _____
5. Write a sentence using the word *parakeet.* _____
   _____
6. The word *paralysis* is what part of speech? _____
7. Write two meanings for *parallel.* _____
   _____
   _____
8. How many words have three syllables? _____
9. What is another word for *parakeet?* _____
10. Write a sentence using the word *parade.* _____
    _____

What a Catch!

Name _____ Date _____

Color the ball that shows the meaning of the underlined word.

1. Dana dove to catch the <u>ball</u> before it hit the ground.
   - (a) **ball** *noun* A round object used in games
   - (b) **ball** *noun* A large, fancy party

2. Bryant makes yummy pancake <u>batter</u>.
   - (a) **batter** *noun* The player whose turn it is to bat
   - (b) **batter** *noun* A flour mixture used to make foods

3. The campers rushed to <u>pitch</u> their tents before dark.
   - (a) **pitch** *verb* To throw the ball to the batter
   - (b) **pitch** *verb* To set up or make ready

4. Mom said she would go on <u>strike</u> if we didn't keep our rooms clean.
   - (a) **strike** *noun* A work stoppage done in order to get better conditions
   - (b) **strike** *noun* A pitch swung at but missed

5. Juan took a <u>swing</u> at the piñata in hope of getting the candy inside.
   - (a) **swing** *noun* A sweeping motion
   - (b) **swing** *noun* A hanging seat that can move back and forth

6. My dad's <u>field</u> is chemistry.
   - (a) **field** *noun* A large piece of treeless land
   - (b) **field** *noun* An area of study or interest

7. Alisa quickly wrapped her brother's gift before he could <u>catch</u> her.
   - (a) **catch** *verb* To find unexpectedly
   - (b) **catch** *verb* To stop something in motion by grabbing with your hands

8. Will's dad asked him to clear the ice off the <u>walk</u>.
   - (a) **walk** *noun* A space meant for people to stroll on
   - (b) **walk** *verb* To move on foot

9. Jamal's aunt is a carpenter by <u>trade</u>.
   - (a) **trade** *verb* To exchange one item for another
   - (b) **trade** *noun* A type of work done

10. Lisa's mom got a <u>diamond</u> necklace for her birthday.
    - (a) **diamond** *noun* A shiny mineral
    - (b) **diamond** *noun* The area on a ball field within the lines that connect the bases

I've got it!

Dictionary: finding meaning **95**

The Hippo Hop

Name _____ Date _____

Use the entries below to find the meaning of the underlined word.

---

¹beat ('bēt) *noun* A pounding sound or rhythm, usually in music

²beat ('bēt) *verb* To win or defeat

¹dance ('dans) *noun* 1. Certain steps done in time to music 2. A party or gathering where people dance

²dance ('dans) *verb* To move one's body or feet in time to music

¹step ('step) *noun* A series of movements done in sequence while dancing or walking

²step ('step) *verb* To raise the foot and put it down in a new position

¹tap ('tap) *noun* A metal piece placed on the bottom of a shoe for tap dancing

²tap ('tap) *verb* To strike gently

---

① Last night, Holly and I <u>danced</u> in the Hippo Hop Dance Contest.

_____

② To get ready for the dance, we had new <u>taps</u> put on our shoes.

_____

③ To start the <u>dance</u>, the Hungry Hippo Band played a new tune.

_____

④ We <u>tapped</u> our feet to the rhythm of the new song.

_____

_____

⑤ Holly liked it, so we <u>stepped</u> onto the floor.

_____

_____

⑥ We both began moving to the <u>beat</u>.

_____

_____

⑦ Then we made dance <u>steps</u> for the new tune.

_____

_____

⑧ Holly and I began doing the Happy Hippo <u>dance</u>.

_____

_____

⑨ Then the judge announced that we <u>beat</u> the other dancers.

_____

_____

Synonym Sort

Name _____   Date _____

Read the thesaurus entries at the top of the page.
Choose the best word to replace the underlined word in the sentence.
Cross out the underlined word and write the new word on the line.

beat *verb* defeat, win

cut *verb* slice, reduce

find *verb* detect, recover

finish *verb* complete, stop

go *verb* leave, withdraw

idea *noun* opinion, belief

like *verb* admire, enjoy

say *verb* declare, recite

take *verb* carry, select

want *verb* desire, lack

1. Did Dan <u>say</u> that he was starting the meeting?

   _____

2. Dora was told to <u>take</u> the box to Duck Express.

   _____

3. During break, Dora tried to <u>beat</u> Dena at cards.

   _____

4. Dena wants to <u>cut</u> the number of hours she works.

   _____

5. Davis had an <u>idea</u> about the new warehouse.

   _____

6. Daisy said she would <u>like</u> going with Dan to the concert.

   _____

7. Davis tried to <u>find</u> where the strange sound was coming from.

8. Devin said he had to <u>finish</u> the details for the workers' picnic.

   _____

9. After the meeting, Dale was ready to <u>go</u>.

   _____

10. Dana said she may <u>want</u> some homemade ice cream.

Thinking It Over

Name _____ Date _____

Use the thesaurus entries to write the best synonym to complete the sentence.
Cross off each synonym after you use it.

give
verb donate, provide, present

see
verb observe, watch, notice

happy
adj. glad, joyful, pleased

good
adj. fine, excellent, pleasant

1) Fran wanted to _____ her lily pads instead of selling them.
   give

2) I was _____ with the way my new lily pad looked.
   happy

3) The sun was warm, and the water was _____ and cool.
   good

4) Flo, did you _____ the new frogs at the pond?
   see

5) We had such an _____ time at the pond, I didn't want to come home!
   good

6) The frogs gave a _____ shout when they learned they won the contest.
   happy

7) Her teacher, Mrs. Frog, wanted to _____ an award to her.
   give

8) We wanted to be there to _____ her receive her award.
   see

9) I was _____ that we weren't late for the final frog dance.
   happy

10) He said it would be _____ for us to look at his fly collection.
    good

11) Frank's mom wanted to _____ the class with snacks for the party.
    give

12) We asked whether we could _____ the tiny tadpoles.
    see

Thesaurus: word connotations

Parent Communication and Student Checkups

Parent Communication and Student Checkups

Table of Contents

Both checkups can be given at the same time, or Checkup B can be given as a follow-up test for students who did not do well on Checkup A. The checkups will help you determine which students have mastered a skill and which students may need more practice.

Great aim!

_____
student

is right on target with

_____!
skill

_____
teacher

_____
date

You hit the bull's-eye!

_____
student

hit the mark with

_____!
skill

_____
teacher

_____
date

It's Time to Take Aim!

On _____ our class will be having a checkup on **synonyms and antonyms.**
To help your child prepare, please spend about 15 minutes reviewing this skill.

Skill Refresher

Hide the answers at the bottom of the page. Guide your child through the definitions and examples below. Then have him complete problems 1–6.

- **Synonyms** are two or more words that mean almost the same thing.

  giant—huge
  vanish—disappear
  injure—hurt
  smell—odor

- **Antonyms** are two words with opposite meanings.

  enter—exit
  rough—smooth
  depart—arrive
  buy—sell

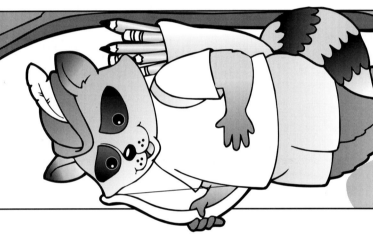

Target These!

Use the word bank to write a synonym for each word.

1. safe _____
2. piece _____

Use the word bank to write an antonym for each word.

3. enemy _____
4. fact _____

Use the word bank to write one synonym and one antonym for each word.

5. glad _____
6. neat _____

| fiction | messy | part | secure |
| happy | friend | tidy | sad |

Answers:

1. secure
2. part
3. friend
4. fiction
5. happy, sad
6. tidy, messy

Checkup 1

Name _____ Date _____

Use the word bank to write a synonym for each word.

1. postpone _____ 2. divide _____

3. donate _____ 4. steal _____

Use the word bank to write an antonym for each word.

5. buy _____ 6. simple _____

7. east _____ 8. crooked _____

Use the word bank to write one synonym and one antonym for each word.

9. alike _____

10. ask _____

straight	give	question	same
delay	west	different	answer
sell	split	complex	take

Test A: Synonyms and antonyms

Checkup 1

Name _____ Date _____

Use the word bank to write a synonym for each word.

1. quick _____ 2. bad _____

3. scare _____ 4. empty _____

Use the word bank to write an antonym for each word.

5. shaky _____ 6. interesting _____

7. fail _____ 8. together _____

Use the word bank to write one synonym and one antonym for each word.

9. under _____

10. listen _____

steady	awful	rapid	apart
boring	above	hear	ignore
vacant	terrify	below	pass

Test B: Synonyms and antonyms

It's Time to Take Aim!

On _____ our class will be having a checkup on **homophones.** To help your child prepare, please spend about 15 minutes reviewing this skill.

Skill Refresher

Hide the answers at the bottom of the page. Guide your child through the definition and examples below. Then have him complete problems 1–8.

Homophones: two or three words that have different spellings and different meanings but are pronounced the same way

its, it's

The dog scratched <u>its</u> ear.

<u>It's</u> time to get a new flea collar.

night, knight

A <u>knight</u> is a medieval soldier.

<u>Night</u> is the time between sundown and sunrise.

Target These!

Circle the homophone that completes each sentence.

1. I had to decide _____ or not to go swimming. (weather/whether)

2. After I visit Jenny and Sophie, _____ going to come to my house. (there, their, they're)

3. Seth feels _____ because he has been sick. (weak, week)

4. _____ you meet me for lunch? (Wood, Would)

Circle the homophone that is incorrect. Write the correct homophone on the line.

5. Phil has three more daze to finish his project. _____

6. Its hard to get to the zoo. _____

7. Don't forget to bring you're homework back. _____

8. Tammy and Josh forgot they're lunches. _____

Answers:

1. whether
2. they're
3. weak
4. Would
5. (daze) days
6. (Its) It's
7. (you're) your
8. (they're) their

Checkup 2

Name _____ Date _____

Circle the homophone that completes each sentence.

1. Ty couldn't get the _____ in his shoelace untied. (knot, not)

2. Mr. and Mrs. Timms brought _____ puppy to the game. (their, they're, there)

3. Is that a new _____ of shoes? (pair, pear)

4. _____ make it to the top if you keep trying. (You'll, Yule)

Circle the homophone that is incorrect.
Write the correct homophone on the line.

5. Shane mist the bus this morning. _____

6. This note doesn't make scents. _____

7. Hour family has two cats and a dog. _____

8. If you eight all of the cookies, you would be sick. _____

Checkup 2

Name _____ Date _____

Circle the homophone that completes each sentence.

1. _____ have to work all day to finish the paper. (Heal, He'll, Heel)

2. I can't remember _____ I put my glasses. (ware, where, wear)

3. This tea is too _____ for me. (suite, sweet)

4. We are number _____! (won, one)

Circle the homophone that is incorrect.
Write the correct homophone on the line.

5. The bird flew in threw the open window. _____

6. Chad cut the bored two inches too short. _____

7. When is your ant Ellen coming to visit? _____

8. Right your name at the top. _____

It's Time to Take Aim!

On _____ our class will be having a checkup on **easily confused words**. To help your child prepare, please spend about 15 minutes reviewing this skill.

Skill Refresher

Hide the answers at the bottom of the page. Guide your child through the definition and examples below. Then have him complete problems 1–8.

Some words sound and look similar and can be **easily confused** or misused.

accept—except	bring—take
than—then	desert—dessert
lose—loose	good—well
close—clothes	angle—angel
all together—altogether	pitcher—picture
quit—quite—quiet	set—sit
lay—lie	breathe—breath
all ready—already	chose—choose

Target These!

Circle the word that correctly completes the sentence.

1. I like to eat pie for (desert, dessert).

2. Mike thinks we will (lose, loose) the game.

3. In geometry, we are learning about right (angles, angels).

4. Sarah did very (good, well) on the test.

5. She failed because she (quite, quit) trying.

6. Let's sing a song (altogether, all together).

7. My brother is taller (than, then) me.

8. I am short of (breathe, breath) from running.

Answers:

1. dessert
2. lose
3. angles
4. well
5. quit
6. all together
7. than
8. breath

©The Education Center, Inc. • *Target Reading & Writing Success* • TEC60877

Checkup 3

Name _____ Date _____

Circle the word that correctly completes the sentence.

1. Please (accept, except) my apology.

2. He worked harder on the project (than, then) she did.

3. The (picture, pitcher) is warming up for the game.

4. We are going shopping for school (close, clothes).

5. The chicken did not (lay, lie) any eggs today.

6. Did you finish your homework (already, all ready)?

7. My sister (choose, chose) not to go to the park.

8. We recently visited the Arizona (dessert, desert).

9. Josh asked me to (sit, set) my tray on the table.

10. Wendy did a (well, good) job on her project.

Test A: Easily confused words

Checkup 3

Name _____ Date _____

Circle the word that correctly completes the sentence.

1. Max finished his chores and (than, then) went out to play.

2. My front tooth is coming (loose, lose).

3. Our teacher asked us to be very (quite, quiet).

4. I took a (pitcher, picture) of my new puppy.

5. After eating lunch, I didn't feel so (good, well).

6. Tom asked us to (clothes, close) the garage door.

7. I think I behaved like an (angle, angel) today.

8. Please (bring, take) me a glass of water.

9. I like all candy (accept, except) lollipops.

10. Diane is dressed and (all ready, already) to go.

Test B: Easily confused words

It's Time to Take Aim!

On _____ our class will be having a checkup on **multiple-meaning words.**
To help your child prepare, please spend about 15 minutes reviewing this skill.

Skill Refresher

Hide the answers at the bottom of the page. Guide your child through the definition and examples below. Then have him complete problems 1–4.

Multiple-meaning words are words that have more than one meaning.

fan	person who likes and supports something
fan	something that cools the air
fair	pleasant
fair	a market
yard	unit of measurement
yard	the area around a house
hard	very firm
hard	difficult

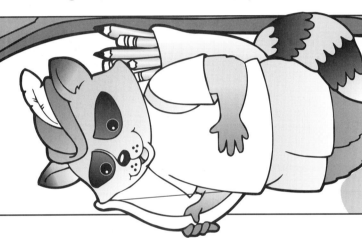

Target These!

Circle the word that completes both sentences.

1. The house was _____ .
    I hurried to _____ the door for him.
    a. open   b. empty   c. pretty

2. I need to _____ our lunch.
    I put the papers on my desk in _____ .
    a. get   b. piles   c. order

Circle the correct meaning of the underlined word.

3. He poured some tea from the <u>pitcher.</u>
    a. baseball player
    b. container for holding liquid

4. I put some food in the fish <u>tank.</u>
    a. large container
    b. vehicle used in battle

Answers:
1. a. open
2. c. order
3. b. container for holding liquid
4. a. large container

Checkup 4

Name _____ Date _____

Use the same word in both blanks to complete each sentence. Use the word bank.

check	left	chest

1. I _____ my coat in the room on the _____.
2. He carried the treasure _____ close to his _____.
3. She wanted to _____ to see whether my _____ had the right amount.

Circle the meaning of the underlined word.

4. Tom pushed the <u>stick</u> into the ground.
   a. to remain or stay   b. twig or branch
5. My <u>back</u> is sore today.
   a. rear part of the body behind the chest   b. to go in reverse
6. What did the sign <u>mean</u>?
   a. to intend to indicate   b. not nice

Circle the word that matches both definitions.

7. to write or spell a word's letters in correct order
   words that have magic power
   a. chant   b. spell   c. list
8. instrument used for writing
   area where animals are kept
   a. pencil   b. fence   c. pen

Test A: Multiple-meaning words

©The Education Center, Inc. • *Target Reading & Writing Success* • TEC60877 • Key p. 136

Checkup 4

Name _____ Date _____

Use the same word in both blanks to complete each sentence. Use the word bank.

story	long	fan

1. I _____ to go to the beach and stay for a _____ time.
2. The baseball _____ began to _____ because she was hot.
3. Her _____ was about a spooky three-story house.

Circle the correct meaning of the underlined word.

4. I need to <u>count</u> the money.
   a. nobleman   b. to name in order
5. She just opened a new law <u>firm</u>.
   a. type of business   b. very hard
6. I tried to <u>spot</u> him in the crowd.
   a. to see   b. certain place

Circle the word that matches both definitions.

7. unit of time
   coming after the first
   a. minute   b. next   c. second
8. certain type
   nice, friendly
   a. brand   b. kind   c. sweet

Test B: Multiple-meaning words

©The Education Center, Inc. • *Target Reading & Writing Success* • TEC60877 • Key p. 136

It's Time to Take Aim!

On _____ our class will be having a checkup on **prefixes**. To help your child prepare, please spend about 15 minutes reviewing this skill.

Skill Refresher

Hide the answers at the bottom of the page. Guide your child through the definitions and examples below. Then have him complete problems 1–8.

A **prefix** is a word part that is added to the beginning of a base word. Prefixes change the meanings of base words.

non- means without
<u>non</u>sense = not making sense

pre- means before
<u>pre</u>view = view before

dis-, im-, in-, un- means not
<u>dis</u>honest = not honest

re- means again
<u>re</u>write = write again

sub- means under
<u>sub</u>soil = under the soil

tri- means three
<u>tri</u>colored = having three colors

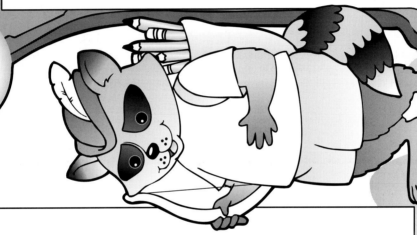

Target These!

Match each meaning to a word from the word bank.

nonstop	subset
disagree	preapproved

1. without stopping _____

2. approved before _____

3. not agree _____

4. under another set _____

Use a prefix to form a new word that matches each definition.

5. not fiction _____

6. not patient _____

7. not measurable _____

8. a ship that travels under water _____

Answers:

1. nonstop
2. preapproved
3. disagree
4. subset
5. nonfiction
6. impatient
7. immeasurable
8. submarine

©The Education Center, Inc. • Target Reading & Writing Success • TEC60877

Checkup 5

Name _____ Date _____

Match each meaning to a word from the word bank.

| displaced | inedible | preview |
| rediscover | nonsense | |

1. discover again _____

2. out of place _____

3. not sensible _____

4. can't be eaten _____

5. view before _____

Use a prefix to make a new word that matches each definition.

6. to claim again _____

7. not polite _____

8. soil that is under the surface _____

9. not sure _____

10. made in advance _____

Test A: Prefixes

Checkup 5

Name _____ Date _____

Match each meaning to a word from the word bank.

| displeased | substructure | untidy |
| recombine | indestructible | |

1. not tidy _____

2. not pleased _____

3. supporting part of a structure _____

4. not capable of being destroyed _____

5. combine again _____

Use a prefix to make a word that matches each definition.

6. having three colors _____

7. to pack again _____

8. not refundable _____

9. to not have been touched _____

10. within or under another set _____

Test B: Prefixes

It's Time to Take Aim!

On _____ our class will be having a checkup on **suffixes**. To help your child prepare, please spend about 15 minutes reviewing this skill.

Skill Refresher

Hide the answers at the bottom of the page. Guide your child through the definition and examples below. Then have him complete problems 1–8.

A **suffix** is a word part that is added to the end of a base word. Suffixes change the meanings of base words.

-ful means "full of"
hope<u>ful</u> = full of hope

-able means "able to"
bend<u>able</u> = able to bend

-less means "without"
home<u>less</u> = without a home

-ness means "state of being"
kind<u>ness</u> = state of being kind

-ly means "in the manner of"
happi<u>ly</u> = in a happy manner

-er means "one who"
bak<u>er</u> = one who bakes

-tion means "the act of"
reac<u>tion</u> = the act of reacting

-ist means "one who"
art<u>ist</u> = one who makes art

Target These!

Form a new word by adding a suffix to match the definition.

tour	dispose
proud	ecology

_____ 1. in a proud manner

_____ 2. one who studies ecology

_____ 3. able to be disposed of

_____ 4. one who tours

Use a suffix from the list at the left to form a new word that matches the definition.

_____ 5. the act of protecting

_____ 6. in a smooth manner

_____ 7. able to be accepted

_____ 8. full of cheer

Answers:

1. proudly
2. ecologist
3. disposable
4. tourist
5. protection
6. smoothly
7. acceptable
8. cheerful

Checkup 6

Name _____ Date _____

Form a new word by adding a suffix to match the definition.

| communicate | clean | wash |
| penny | biology | |

1. one who studies biology _____

2. the act of communicating _____

3. without pennies _____

4. one who cleans _____

5. able to be washed _____

Use a suffix to form a new word that matches the definition.

6. full of delight _____

7. state of being kind _____

8. in a hungry manner _____

9. one who studies science _____

10. the act of locating _____

Test A: Suffixes

Checkup 6

Name _____ Date _____

Form a new word by adding a suffix to match the definition.

| spot | organize | neat |
| teach | beauty | |

1. one who teaches _____

2. without spots _____

3. full of beauty _____

4. the act of organizing _____

5. in a neat manner _____

Use a suffix to form a new word that matches the definition.

6. state of being weak _____

7. able to be cured _____

8. one who studies biology _____

9. able to be accepted _____

10. the act of protecting _____

Test B: Suffixes

It's Time to Take Aim!

On _____ our class will be having a checkup on **base words.**
To help your child prepare, please spend about 15 minutes reviewing this skill.

Skill Refresher

Hide the answers at the bottom of the page. Guide your child through the definitions and examples below. Then have him complete problems 1–6.

A **base word** is a word in its simplest form. When prefixes and/or suffixes are added to a base word, the word's meaning changes.

pre + **arrange** + ment = the result of arranging in advance

re + **pay** + able = able to be paid again

Target These!

Write each word's base.

1. dissatisfaction _____

2. pretreatment _____

3. unhappiness _____

4. inaction _____

Write each word's prefix, base, and suffix. Then write the word's meaning.

5. unlikely

_____ + _____ + _____ =

_____

6. unreadable

_____ + _____ + _____ =

_____

Answers:

1. satisfy
2. treat
3. happy
4. act
5. un + like + ly = in a way that is not likely
6. un + read + able = not able to be read

Checkup 7

Name _____ Date _____

Write each word's base.

1. inaction _____

2. nonpayment _____

3. renewable _____

4. unhappily _____

5. indigestion _____

6. colorless _____

Write each word's prefix, base, and suffix. Then write the word's meaning.

7. repayable _____ + _____ + _____ = _____

8. unreasonable _____ + _____ + _____ = _____

9. disagreement _____ + _____ + _____ = _____

10. unbelievable _____ + _____ + _____ = _____

©The Education Center, Inc. • *Target Reading & Writing Success* • TEC60877 • Key p. 136

Checkup 7

Name _____ Date _____

Write each word's base.

1. prepay _____

2. uncomfortable _____

3. pretreatment _____

4. disagreeable _____

5. prearrangement _____

6. unbreakable _____

Write each word's prefix, base, and suffix. Then write the word's meaning.

7. nonparticipation _____ + _____ + _____ = _____

8. disrespectful _____ + _____ + _____ = _____

9. unreadable _____ + _____ + _____ = _____

10. unlikely _____ + _____ + _____ = _____

©The Education Center, Inc. • *Target Reading & Writing Success* • TEC60877 • Key p. 136

It's Time to Take Aim!

On _____ our class will be having a checkup on **Greek roots.**
To help your child prepare, please spend about 15 minutes reviewing this skill.

Skill Refresher

Hide the answers at the bottom of the page. Guide your child through the rules and examples below. Then have him complete problems 1–8.

Some words have word parts from other languages. Many words have Greek roots. The following are some examples:

arch = chief or ruler

aster, astr = star

auto = self

bio = life

chron = time

cycl = circle

geo = earth

gram = thing written

graph = writing

hydr = water

mech = machine

meter = measure

micro = small

mono = one

phon = sound

photo = light

sphere = ball

tele = far off

therm = heat

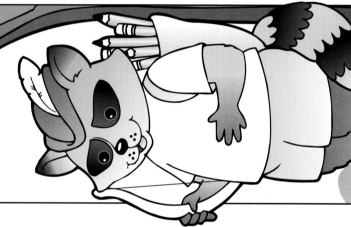

Target These!

Circle each Greek root in the words below.

1. mechanical
2. micrometer
3. diagram
4. perimeter
5. telegram

Match each meaning to a word from the word bank.

| thermometer   autograph   biography |

6. the story of a person's life _____

7. an instrument that measures temperature _____

8. a person's signature _____

Answers:
1. mech anical
2. micro meter
3. dia gram
4. peri meter
5. tele gram
6. biography
7. thermometer
8. autograph

Checkup 8

Name _____ Date _____

Circle the common Greek root in each word below.

1. calligraphy
2. bicycle
3. astronomy
4. photocopier
5. architect

6. thermostat
7. cyclone
8. hydraulic
9. asterisk
10. atmosphere

Match each meaning to a word from the word bank.

| monarch | mechanic | perimeter | hemisphere | telescope |

_____ 11. half of the earth or another sphere

_____ 12. a person who fixes machines

_____ 13. the king or queen of a country

_____ 14. an instrument used for looking at stars

_____ 15. the length around an area

Test A: Greek roots

Checkup 8

Name _____ Date _____

Circle the common Greek root(s) in the words below.

1. program
2. monochromatic
3. patriarch
4. biopsy
5. photocell

6. mechanism
7. thermal
8. telephone
9. thermos
10. grammar

Match each meaning to a word from the word bank.

| asteroid | hydrant | recycle | automobile | symphony |

_____ 11. car

_____ 12. to use again and again

_____ 13. a large orchestra

_____ 14. a small body that revolves around the sun

_____ 15. a large water pipe in the ground, used by firefighters to put out fires

Test B: Greek roots

It's Time to Take Aim!

On _____ our class will be having a checkup on **Latin word roots.**
To help your child prepare, please spend about 15 minutes reviewing this skill.

Skill Refresher

Hide the answers at the bottom of the page. Guide your child through the examples below. Then have him complete problems 1–10.

Some words have word parts from other languages. Many words have Latin roots. The following are some examples of latin roots:

ped = foot

fin = end

aud = to hear

rupt = to break

scrib = to write

man = hand

mob = to move

min = to make smaller

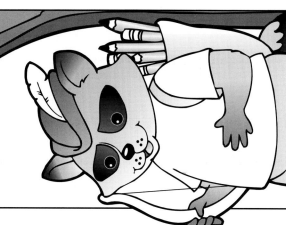

Target These!

Circle the Latin root in the words below.

1. diminish
2. manufacture
3. scribble
4. finale
5. audition

Match each meaning to a word from the word bank.

| audible | erupt | pedometer |
| mobility | minimum | |

6. the least amount _____
7. to burst out _____
8. able to be heard _____
9. a tool that measures the number of steps taken _____
10. the state of being able to move _____

Answers:

1. di(min)ish
2. (man)ufacture
3. (scrib)ble
4. (fin)ale
5. (aud)ition
6. minimum
7. erupt
8. audible
9. pedometer
10. mobility

Checkup 9

Name _____ Date _____

Circle the Latin root in the words below.

1. minute
2. subscribe
3. finish
4. manual
5. demobilize
6. interrupt
7. prescription
8. centipede
9. minnow
10. audio

Match each meaning to a word from the word bank.

infinite	diminish	manuscript	abrupt	centipede

11. _____ to make smaller

12. _____ sudden

13. _____ without end

14. _____ written by hand

15. _____ creature that seems to have 100 legs

Checkup 9

Name _____ Date _____

Circle the Latin root in the words below.

1. inscribe
2. corrupt
3. minor
4. automobile
5. finale
6. manicure
7. auditory
8. minus
9. transcript
10. pedestal

Match each meaning to a word from the word bank.

describe	pedometer	manager	interrupt	minor

11. _____ lesser

12. _____ to tell in written or spoken words

13. _____ to break into something that is happening

14. _____ one who controls things

15. _____ a tool that measures the number of steps taken

It's Time to Take Aim!

On _____ our class will be having a checkup on **similes and metaphors.**
To help your child prepare, please spend about 15 minutes reviewing this skill.

Skill Refresher

Hide the answers at the bottom of the page. Guide your child through the definitions and examples below. Then have him complete problems 1–8.

- A **simile** compares two unlike things using *like* or *as.*

  He jumped <u>as quick as a cricket.</u>

  The chips were <u>salty like the ocean.</u>

  The baby was <u>as light as a feather.</u>

- A **metaphor** compares two unlike things without using *like* or *as.*

  I was a <u>shining star in art class.</u>

  The line was a <u>snake curled around the building.</u>

  She was a <u>fish swimming through the water.</u>

Target These!

Write *S* or *M* to identify each underlined phrase as a simile or a metaphor.

____ 1. He was <u>an angry lion</u> when he missed dinner.

____ 2. Her eyes <u>sparkled like diamonds.</u>

____ 3. He was <u>as tall as a giraffe.</u>

Complete each well-known simile or metaphor with a word from the word bank.

| swan   turtle   thunder |

4. Their voices were as loud as _____ .

5. She was a graceful _____ dancing on the stage.

6. He was as slow as a _____ .

Complete each simile or metaphor.

7. The girl was as quiet as _____ .

8. My hair is a _____ .

Answers:

1. M
2. S
3. S

4. thunder
5. swan
6. turtle

7. Answers will vary.
8. Answers will vary.

©The Education Center, Inc. • *Target Reading & Writing Success* • TEC60877

120

Checkup 10

Name _____ Date _____

Write *S* or *M* to identify each underlined phrase as a simile or a metaphor.

____ 1. The window was <u>as shiny as a new penny.</u>

____ 2. The sunflowers <u>were tall soldiers</u> in the sunshine.

____ 3. Matt was <u>as warm as toast</u> in his new jacket.

____ 4. The kite <u>was an eagle</u> soring in the sky.

Complete each well-known simile or metaphor with a word from the word bank.

bird   monkeys   honey

5. The children chattered like _____ .

6. The snacks were as sweet as _____ .

7. She sang like a _____ .

Complete each simile or metaphor.

8. Mark's feet were as cold as _____ .

9. Susan was as proud as _____ .

10. The chocolate cake was _____ .

©The Education Center, Inc. • *Target Reading & Writing Success* • TEC60877 • Key p. 136

Test A: Similes and metaphors

Checkup 10

Name _____ Date _____

Write *S* or *M* to identify each underlined phrase as a simile or a metaphor.

____ 1. She was <u>as pretty as a picture</u> in her new dress.

____ 2. Her fingers were <u>cold icicles.</u>

____ 3. The baby <u>was a quiet mouse</u> while waiting for her bottle.

____ 4. Deion was <u>as busy as a bee</u> at his new job.

Complete each well-known simile or metaphor with a word from the word bank.

sandpaper   bell   cheetah

5. His voice was as clear as a _____ when he spoke.

6. The runner was a fast _____ on the track.

7. That fabric was as rough as _____ .

Complete each simile or metaphor.

8. The baby's skin is as soft as _____ .

9. Her eyes were _____ .

10. The road was as bumpy as _____ .

©The Education Center, Inc. • *Target Reading & Writing Success* • TEC60877 • Key p. 136

Test B: Similes and metaphors

It's Time to Take Aim!

On _____ our class will be having a checkup on **idioms, onomatopoeia, alliteration, and hyperbole.** To help your child prepare, please spend about 15 minutes reviewing this skill.

Skill Refresher

Hide the answers at the bottom of the page. Guide your child through the definitions and examples below. Then have him complete problems 1–8.

- **Idioms** are sayings whose meanings differ from the meanings of the individual words.
  I felt fit as a fiddle after the hike.

- **Onomatopoeia** is using words that sound like sounds.
  The bees buzzed in the garden.

- **Alliteration** is using together two or more words that begin with the same sound.
  Annie ate apples this afternoon.

- **Hyperbole** is using exaggeration to make a point.
  I'm so tired I could sleep for a month!

Target These!

Write *I, O, A,* or *H* to identify each underlined phrase as an idiom, onomatopoeia, alliteration, or hyperbole.

____ 1. My feet were frozen solid from walking through the snow.

____ 2. We whooped when we saw who won the game.

____ 3. She used a lot of elbow grease to clean her room.

____ 4. Freddy forgot to fry the fish for his friends.

____ 5. The plate crashed to the ground.

____ 6. It's raining cats and dogs out there!

____ 7. The crispy crackers created lots of crumbs.

____ 8. My mouth was drier than the desert.

Answers:

1. H
2. O
3. I

4. A
5. O
6. I

7. A
8. H

Checkup 11

Name _____   Date _____

Write *I*, *O*, *A*, or *H* to identify each underlined phrase as an idiom,
onomatopoeia, alliteration, or hyperbole.

___ 1. Mike <u>stomped</u> to his room angrily.

___ 2. Those pancakes are <u>bigger than plates</u>!

___ 3. The steak <u>sizzled</u> on the grill.

___ 4. I was <u>in a pickle</u> when I forgot my homework.

___ 5. <u>Peter's painting of the parrot</u> was perfect.

___ 6. The sidewalk was <u>hot enough to fry eggs</u>.

___ 7. I need to <u>spruce up</u> the house before my guests arrive.

___ 8. I was <u>tickled pink</u> when I won the race!

___ 9. The football fans were <u>fascinated by the field</u> goal.

___ 10. Those books <u>weighed a ton</u>.

©The Education Center, Inc. • *Target Reading & Writing Success* • TEC60877 • Key p. 136

Checkup 11

Name _____   Date _____

Write *I*, *O*, *A*, or *H* to identify the underlined phrase as an idiom,
onomatopoeia, alliteration, or hyperbole.

___ 1. <u>John juggled six jars of jam</u>.

___ 2. He was <u>taller than a giraffe</u>!

___ 3. It's time to <u>rise and shine</u>!

___ 4. The cold rain <u>pinged</u> against the window.

___ 5. <u>Frank</u> went to the <u>fall fair on Friday</u>.

___ 6. The dogs began to <u>bark and howl</u>.

___ 7. Your handwriting is <u>so small I need a microscope to read it</u>.

___ 8. That song really <u>gets on my nerves</u>.

___ 9. The birds began to <u>chirp</u> after sunrise.

___ 10. <u>Cole collected seashells at the coast</u>.

©The Education Center, Inc. • *Target Reading & Writing Success* • TEC60877 • Key p. 136

It's Time to Take Aim!

On _____ our class will be having a checkup on some types of **dictionary skills**. To help your child prepare, please spend about 15 minutes reviewing this skill.

Skill Refresher

Hide the answers at the bottom of the page. Guide your child through the definition and example below. Then have him complete problems 1–7.

A **dictionary entry** gives the meaning(s) of a word and often uses the word in a sample sentence. A dictionary also tells you

- how to pronounce the word
- what part of speech it is
- the language the word came from
- other forms of the word

dance ('dans) *verb* 1. To move the body or feet in time to music: *We turned on the radio and danced.* 2. To move about quickly or lightly: *Sunlight danced on the water.* [Middle English] *verb* **danced, dancing;** *noun* **dance;** *noun, plural* **dances**

Target These!

Use the dictionary entry below to answer the questions.

comfortable (kum'•fer•tə•bel) *adjective* 1. Giving comfort or ease: *My new chair was comfortable.* 2. At ease: *After a few days, I felt comfortable there.* [Latin] *adverb* **comfortably**

1. Draw a box around the main entry word.
2. How many syllables are in the word? _____
3. Draw a circle around the pronunciation.
4. Put an X over the part of speech.
5. How many definitions does *comfortable* have? _____
6. Draw a line under the example sentences.
7. Write the other word that is a form of the word *comfortable*. _____

Answers:

comfortable (kum'•fer•tə•bel) ~~adjective~~ 1. Giving comfort or ease: <u>My new chair was comfortable.</u> 2. At ease: <u>After a few days, I felt comfortable there.</u> [Latin] *adverb* **comfortably**

2. 4
5. 2
7. comfortably

Checkup 12

Name _____ Date _____

Use the dictionary entry to answer the questions below.

icy (ī′•sē) *adjective* 1. Covered with or made of ice: *The roads were icy after the storm.* 2. Very cold: *The temperatures were icy in the winter.* 3. Cold and unfriendly: *His attitude toward her was icy.* [Middle English] *adjective* **icier, iciest**

1. Draw a box around the main entry word.

2. How many syllables are in the word? _____

3. Draw a circle around the pronunciation.

4. Put an X over the part of speech.

5. How many definitions does *icy* have? _____

6. Draw a line under the example sentences.

7. Write two other words that are forms of the word *icy.* _____

8. Write a sentence using the word *icy.*

_____

_____

Checkup 12

Name _____ Date _____

Use the dictionary entry to answer the questions below.

aquarium (ə•kwâr′•ē•əm) *noun* 1. A container, such as a tank or bowl, in which fish, other water animals, or water plants are kept: *The fish swam around the aquarium.* 2. A building where collections of fish, other water animals, and water plants are displayed: *We went to the aquarium to see the sharks.* [Latin] *noun, plural* **aquariums**

1. Draw a box around the main entry word.

2. How many syllables are in the word? _____

3. Draw a circle around the pronunciation.

4. Put an X over the part of speech.

5. How many definitions does *aquarium* have? _____

6. Draw a line under the example sentences.

7. Write two words that have the same meaning as *aquarium.* _____

8. Write a sentence using the word *aquarium.*

_____

_____

Student Progress Chart

student		Date	Number Correct	Comments
Checkup 1 Synonyms and Antonyms	A			
	B			
Checkup 2 Homophones	A			
	B			
Checkup 3 Easily Confused Words	A			
	B			
Checkup 4 Multiple-Meaning Words	A			
	B			
Checkup 5 Prefixes	A			
	B			
Checkup 6 Suffixes	A			
	B			

Student Progress Chart

student		Date	Number Correct	Comments
Checkup 7 Base Words	A			
	B			
Checkup 8 Greek Roots	A			
	B			
Checkup 9 Latin Roots	A			
	B			
Checkup 10 Similes and Metaphors	A			
	B			
Checkup 11 Idioms, Onomatopoeia, Hyperbole, and Alliteration	A			
	B			
Checkup 12 Dictionary Skills	A			
	B			

Page 7

1. move
2. mend
3. delay
4. revise
5. pointed
6. grow
7. illegal
8. split
9. wealth
10. secure
11. untidy
12. take
13. ache
14. entire
15. use
16. attempt

IN THE "STORK" MARKET

Page 8

1. error
2. obey
3. vanish
4. raise
5. omit
6. often
7. odor
8. need
9. usual
10. depart
11. terrify
12. give
13. vacant
14. wild
15. vary

Page 9

Color Code

said = orange   good = red
cold = purple   big = yellow
fast = blue   small = green

Page 10

#				
1. mad	**calm**	angry	furious	upset
2. easy	basic	**old**	simple	plain
3. thin	skinny	**sharp**	slim	slender
4. walk	**examine**	stroll	march	trek
5. bad	awful	**scare**	terrible	poor
6. take	snatch	get	**obey**	grab
7. old	antique	used	worn	**angry**
8. new	modern	current	recent	**terrible**
9. quiet	silent	hushed	**sharp**	soundless
10. ask	inquire	question	**give**	quiz
11. wet	soaked	**calm**	soggy	moist
12. hot	**rapid**	sizzling	fiery	heated

Page 11

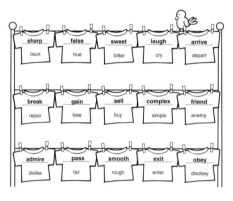

sharp	false	sweet	laugh	arrive
blunt	true	bitter	cry	depart

break	gain	sell	complex	friend
repair	lose	buy	simple	enemy

admire	pass	smooth	exit	obey
dislike	fail	rough	enter	disobey

Page 12

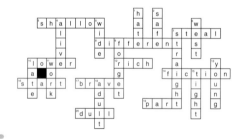

Crossword answers:
shallow, hat, safe, steal, different, rich, lower, fiction, start, brave, part, dull

Page 13

Surfside Private Beach Forecast

~~Public~~

Sunrise Sunset is at 6:05. Today's ~~low~~ **high** temperature will be ~~below~~ **above** normal. The water will be rough and ~~smooth~~ ~~cool~~ **warm**. Sunshine will ~~decrease~~ **increase** throughout the ~~evening~~ **morning**. Showers will ~~depart~~ **arrive** ~~quickly~~ **slowly** from the ~~west~~ **east** and then appear by the ~~beginning~~ **end** of the ~~night~~ **day**.

Beach Rules

Swim to the ~~north~~ **south** of the lifeguard stand. ~~Tame~~ **Wild** animals are ~~legal~~ **illegal** on the beach. No ~~soft~~ **loud** music. Do not walk on the ~~artificial~~ **live** sea plants. Each ~~adult~~ **child** should ~~destroy~~ **build** a sand castle. Never swim ~~without~~ **with** a buddy. Please ~~ignore~~ **follow** all beach rules or you will be ~~rewarded~~ **punished**!

Page 14

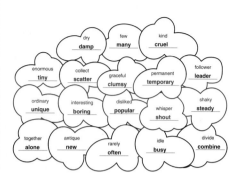

dry — damp, few — many, kind — cruel, enormous — tiny, collect — scatter, graceful — clumsy, permanent — temporary, follower — leader, ordinary — unique, interesting — boring, disliked — popular, whisper — shout, shaky — steady, together — alone, antique — new, rarely — often, idle — busy, divide — combine

Page 15

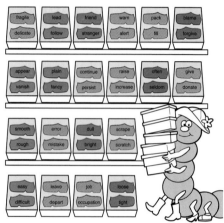

fragile — delicate	lead — follow	friend — stranger	warm — alert	pack — fill	blame — forgive
appear — vanish	plain — fancy	continue — persist	raise — increase	often — seldom	give — donate
smooth — rough	error — mistake	dull — bright	scrape — scratch		
easy — difficult	leave — depart	job — occupation	loose — tight		

Page 16

under — below / above	spotless — clean / dirty	finish — end / beginning	adore — love / hate
listen — hear / ignore	combine — add / subtract	grab — take / give	repair — fix / break
well — healthy / ill	silent — quiet / noisy	tardy — late / early	none — nothing / everything
diverse — different / same	happy — glad / sad	ask — question / answer	tart — sour / sweet

1. side
2. wood
3. I
4. pour or pore
5. flew
6. days
7. knew
8. see
9. night
10. aloud
11. brake
12. pears

A few days ago, Blackbeak found a treasure chest that had washed in from the sea. Blackbeak knew there would be a big bounty inside. He worked all night to pull it out of the water. When he finally pulled it out, he found that it was locked.

Blackbeak said aloud, "I can use my strong beak to break the lock!" The chest flew open and Blackbeak gazed inside. The chest was filled with sweet, juicy pears.

Blackbeak sighed and said, "Well, I'm still poor, but I won't go hungry!"

Page 20

for | **four** | fore
where | ware | wear
road | rode | rowed
heal | **he'll** | heel
merry | Mary | **marry**
carrot | caret | **carat**
raise | **rays** | raze
seas | **sees** | seize
sense | cents | scents
their | they're | there
rein | **reign** | rain
rite | write | **right**

Princess Freida | Princess Fifi | Princess Felice

Page 21

The following words should be circled.
1. grate
2. higher
3. close
4. feat
5. guest
6. grown
7. witch
8. strait
9. here
10. hair
11. patients
12. lessen

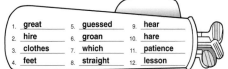

1. **great** 5. **guessed** 9. **hear**
2. **hire** 6. **groan** 10. **hare**
3. **clothes** 7. **which** 11. **patience**
4. **feet** 8. **straight** 12. **lesson**

Page 22

You're Invited!

B Come **won**, come all
S To Pack E. Derm **Peak**
O For a **reel** picnic
N That cannot be **beet**!

Q Be **there** by two,
T Or even ten past the **our**.
U I hope the **sun** shines
R So we can **sea** from the tower.

A Your favorite **sweet** treat
R Is what **ewe** should bring.
I A **guessed** will be welcome,
M Just **knot** a creepy, crawly thing!

S This gathering will be **great**
L **Fore** all of our kin.
P I hope **yule** all come!
H Love, **Aunt** Gray Skin

What game do elephants play with ants?
To answer the riddle, write the letters from the colored cookies in order on the lines below.
S Q U A S H

Page 23

Sentences will vary.

blue | **blew**
the color of the sky

maid | made
a female servant

bored | **board**
a flat piece of wood

creek | creak
a small, winding stream

weak | **week**
a period of seven days

meat | **meet**
to get together

you're | your
contraction of you are

knows | **nose**
the part of the body used for breathing air

Page 24

1. fourth, forth
2. whether, weather
3. mist, missed
4. through, threw
5. not, knot
6. sighed, side
7. It's, its
8. caught, cot
9. eight, ate

Page 25

1. there
2. They're
3. their
4. There
5. there
6. they're
7. their
8. They're
9. there
10. they're
11. Their
12. their
13. their
14. there
15. they're

Page 26

YOU TICKLE IT

Page 27

1. all together
2. close
3. than
4. Except
5. altogether
6. accept
7. then
8. except
9. all together
10. Then
11. close
12. clothes
13. accept
14. close
15. than

Page 28

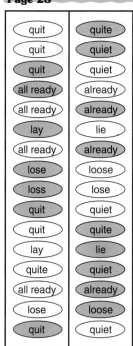

quit | **quite**
quit | **quiet**
quit | quiet
all ready | already
all ready | already
lay | lie
all ready | already
lose | loose
loss | lose
quit | quiet
quit | **quite**
lay | **lie**
quite | **quiet**
all ready | already
lose | **loose**
quit | quiet

THAT H I T THE
S P O T S!

1. seal
2. bank
3. fan
4. point
5. press
6. open
7. face
8. date
9. back
10. like

1. Z
2. D
3. S
4. Z
5. G
6. R
7. B
8. U
9. H
10. A

BUZZARDS

1. mean, mean
2. kind, kind
3. right, right
4. spot, spot
5. hide, hide
6. second, second
7. pen, pen
8. story, story
9. blow, blow
10. spell, spell

1. b
2. a
3. b
4. b
5. b
6. a
7. a
8. b
9. a
10. a

1. S
2. I
3. U
4. A
5. V
6. U
7. T
8. F
9. R
10. E

FIVE-STAR

1. a
2. a
3. b
4. a
5. b
6–10. Sentences will vary.

1. fair
2. park
3. fan
4. trunk
5. cap
6. bat
7. strike
8. watch
9. cry
10. out
11. stands
12. pitcher
13. run
14. land
15. star

B. Did you unpack a <u>case</u> of books?
A. The lawyer took her <u>case</u>.

I. He belongs to a <u>club</u> for boys.
J. I forgot my favorite golf <u>club</u>.

C. <u>Part</u> of the order was not delivered.
D. She played the lead <u>part</u>.

K. I like to <u>dip</u> strawberries in chocolate.
L. Have you tried my new cheese <u>dip</u>?

F. I wanted to <u>rest</u> after the game.
E. The <u>rest</u> of the food will arrive Monday.

N. The new movie is a <u>hit</u>!
M. I <u>hit</u> the ball into the outfield.

G. Could you show me your fish <u>tank</u>?
H. I saw an army <u>tank</u> parked outside.

O. The fish was covered with tiny <u>scales</u>.
P. He weighed himself on two different <u>scales</u>.

R. I lost my car <u>key</u>.
Q. The <u>key</u> to good grades is hard work.

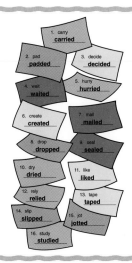

1. carry **carried**
2. pad **padded**
3. decide **decided**
4. wait **waited**
5. hurry **hurried**
6. create **created**
7. mail **mailed**
8. drop **dropped**
9. seal **sealed**
10. dry **dried**
11. like **liked**
12. rely **relied**
13. tape **taped**
14. slip **slipped**
15. jot **jotted**
16. study **studied**

Page 44

in the sand	behind a log	on a boat	in the guitar case
singeing	singging	sinning	**singing**
tunying	tuneing	**tuning**	tunning
struming	strumeing	**strumming**	strummng
croakking	**croaking**	crocking	croking
clicing	clikking	**clicking**	clickeing
arriveing	**arriving**	arrivig	arrivving
tapping	tapeing	taping	tapinng
druming	**drumming**	drumeing	drumying
hurring	**hurrying**	hurying	hurryng
calling	caling	callying	calleing
buzing	**buzzing**	buzzying	buzzig
tacking	takeing	**taking**	takking
swimying	swiming	swimmng	**swimming**
playeing	playying	plaing	**playing**
slithing	slitherring	**slithering**	slitherng
sharring	**sharing**	shareing	sharinng
floating	floatying	floatting	floatingg
celebrateing	**celebrating**	celebratting	celebratng
frettig	freting	**fretting**	freteing
satisfing	**satisfying**	sattisfying	satisffying

Page 45

1. grow
2. water
3. plan
4. fertilize
5. rake
6. add
7. breathe
8. snip
9. climb
10. hoe
11. begin
12. prepare
13. transplant
14. drop
15. live
16. place
Because she wanted richer soil.

likeness
weakness
kindness
politeness
thickness
happiness

enjoyable
washable
disposable
acceptable

spotless
careless
helpless
priceless
endless
penniless

Page 47

1. proudly
2. baker
3. delightful
4. grocer
5. loudly
6. smoothly
7. cheerful
8. happily
9. teacher
10. skillful
11. cleaner
12. hungrily
13. beautiful
14. neatly

Page 48

Answers may vary.
1. conserve + -tion = conservation
   the act of conserving
2. organize + -tion = organization
   the act of organizing
3. biology + -ist = biologist
   one who practices biology
4. locate + -tion = location
   the act of locating
5. tour + -ist = tourist
   one who tours
6. ecology + -ist = ecologist
   one who practices ecology
7. protect + -tion = protection
   the act of protecting
8. science + -ist = scientist
   one who practices science
9. communicate + -tion = communication
   the act of communicating
10. art + -ist = artist
    one who practices art

Gail and Gary are climbing Old Mount Baldy. Gail has practiced climbing for four weeks. So she feels <u>hopeful</u> that she can keep up with Gary. He is two years older and more <u>powerful</u> than Gail. Gail had felt <u>hopeless</u> before she started practicing. But now Gail is sure she can keep up.

Gary and Gail are <u>careful</u> as they climb the peak. If they are <u>careless</u>, they might stumble. Falling would be very <u>painful</u>.

Gail's new water bottle leaks. "It's <u>useless</u>!" she cries. "It would be <u>helpful</u> if I had a water bottle that actually held water." Gary laughs and hands Gail his old beat-up canteen.

While Gail drinks Gary's water, Gary looks around at the <u>endless</u> horizon. Gary announces, "We did it! We are at the top!"

"And look," Gail says, "Now I know why it's called Old Mount Baldy. It's completely <u>treeless</u>!"

Page 50

1. nonsense
2. prehistoric
3. rechew
4. reclaimed
5. nonedible
6. repack
7. nonstop
8. preapproved
9. prefilled
10. premade
11. rediscover
12. nonfiction
13. preview
14. premeasure
15. recombine

Page 51

1. L
2. A
3. E
4. N
5. M
6. P
7. C
8. K
9. S
10. R
11. U
12. D
13. T
14. I

SNEAKERS

Page 52

triangle	rectangle	square
bicycle	unicycle	tricycle
nation	bisect	bistate
brace	trilogy	tripod
unify	bifocal	bivalve
unicorn	uniform	zephyr
triweekly	trilogy	trio
tricky	triple	tribute
uni-level	bi-level	tri-level
triumph	tribute	trio
English	unilingual	bilingual
binocular	bimonthly	semiannual
triceratops	brontosaur	stegosaurus
molar	bicuspid	premolar
colorful	tricolor	triplicate

All balls should be colored.

1. unknown
2. unclear
3. inactive
4. immeasurable
5. untouched
6. unsure
7. independent
8. inedible
9. uneven
10. imperfect
11. indestructible
12. unlock
13. impatient
14. impolite
15. inexpensive
16. incomplete

new
act
read
respect
break
happy
satisfy
reason
digest
pay
place
migrate

THEY HEARD SOMEONE WAS STEALING BASES

1. non + participate + ion
   the act of not participating
2. un + break + able
   not able to break
3. pre + treat + ment
   the act of treating before
4. un + comfort + able
   not able to have comfort
5. un + believe + able
   not able to be believed
6. pre + arrange + ment
   the act of arranging before
7. non + pay + ment
   the act of not paying

Answers for the first section may vary.
Possible answers include the following:
happy: unhappy, happily, happiness,
   unhappiness, unhappily
agree: disagree, agreeable, agreement,
   disagreeable, disagreement,
   agreeably, disagreeably
pay: prepay, payable, repay, payment,
   repayable, repayment
color: uncolor, colorful, colorless,
   discolor, colorable
care: careful, careless, carefully,
   carelessness, carelessly
like: likable, likely, likeness, unlikely,
   dislikable

1. unhappily
2. disagreeable
3. prepay
4. colorless
5. carefully
6. unlikely

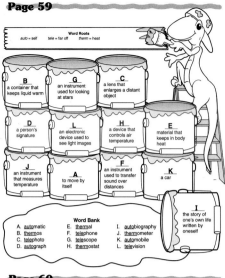

Word Roots
auto = self   tele = far off   therm = heat

B. a container that keeps liquid warm
G. an instrument used for looking at stars
C. a lens that enlarges a distant object
D. a person's signature
L. an electronic device used to see light images
H. a device that controls air temperature
E. material that keeps in body heat
J. an instrument that measures temperature
A. to move by itself
F. an instrument used to transfer sound over distances
K. a car
I. the story of one's own life written by oneself

Word Bank
A. automatic
B. thermos
C. telephoto
D. autograph
E. thermal
F. telephone
G. telescope
H. thermostat
I. autobiography
J. thermometer
K. automobile
L. television

Tonight's Symphony Performance
A. Recycle
B. Biography
C. Bicycle
D. Telegraph
E. Synchronized
F. Telephone
G. Cyclone
H. Chronology

• Phil, our photographer, for taking pictures of the event.
• Carmen, for writing the program in calligraphy.

Telephone
Chronology
photographer
Recycle
Synchronized
Biography
calligraphy
Bicycle
Telegraph
Symphony
Cyclone

Order of answers may vary.
hydrant
hydroplane
hydroelectric
hydraulic
hydrate
Word root: hydr
Meaning: water

photograph
telephoto
photocell
photocopier
photosynthesis
Word root: photo
Meaning: light

astronaut
astrology
astronomy
asterisk
asteroid
Word root: astr
Meaning: star

chief or ruler
root: arch
patriarch
architect
anarchy
hierarchy
archangel
monarch

life
root: bio
antibiotic
biome
biology
symbiotic
biopsy
biography

earth
root: geo
geography
geode
geocentric
geometry
geothermal
geology

	Yes	No
mechanic	S	A
monologue	C	T
micrometer	E	D
mechanical	T	C
microscope	I	S
microcomputer	O	L
monochromatic	S	T
microphone	R	A
microwave	V	I
mechanism	O	H

DO HAT TRICKS

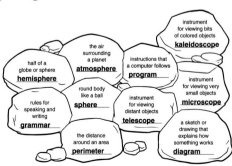

instrument for viewing bits of colored objects **kaleidoscope**
the air surrounding a planet **atmosphere**
instructions that a computer follows **program**
half of a globe or sphere **hemisphere**
instrument for viewing very small objects **microscope**
round body like a ball **sphere**
instrument for viewing distant objects **telescope**
rules for speaking and writing **grammar**
the distance around an area **perimeter**
a sketch or drawing that explains how something works **diagram**

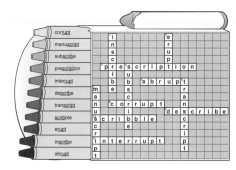

corrupt
manuscript
subscribe
prescription
interrupt
describe
scribble
erupt
inscribe
abrupt

Orders of answers may vary.

popular
population
populate
popularity
unpopular

maneuver
manual
manager
manufactured
manicure
manipulate

multiply
multimedia
multitude
multiple
multicolor

		Yes	No
1.	centipede	A	L
2.	auditorium	N	C
3.	moped	A	T
4.	audition	L	D
5.	audible	T	S
6.	pedicure	E	S
7.	pedestal	F	G
8.	auditory	M	F
9.	audiotape	K	E
10.	pedometer	O	A

FANS ALL LEFT

1. tractor
2. extract
3. tracks
4. distracted
5. trace
6. sport
7. portable
8. support
9. reporter
10. transported
11. suspected
12. spectacles
13. inspect
14. expected

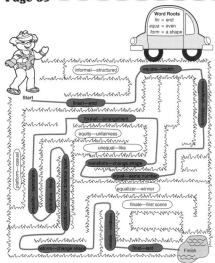

Word Roots
fin = end
equa = even
form = a shape

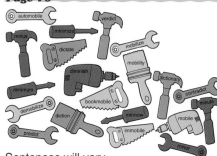

Sentences will vary.

4 — an accomplishment or honor

8 — there is no limit on what can be achieved

1 — unimportant, not worth anything

3 — to be very happy and excited

10 — be careful with what is said or done

7 — taking a chance on a single thing or idea

2 — an early start gives a better chance of success

5 — escape or go away suddenly

6 — cause trouble

9 — help or guide someone

1. F
2. E
3. A
4. T
5. O
6. D
7. R
8. W
9. S
10. B

BEST FOOT FORWARD

A. Rodney had butterflies in his stomach before attempting the trick.
B. He couldn't put his finger on why he was having trouble.
C. Rodney knew he could do it, but he had to keep his chin up!
D. He started to think he was wet behind the ears when it came to skating.
E. Rodney was all ears as his friend told him he just needed a new skateboard.
F. A new skateboard would cost an arm and a leg!
G. Maybe he could clean and repair his old one with some elbow grease.
H. Rodney put his foot down and decided that he was going to do the trick.
I. He said, "Keep your eyes peeled for my next trick!"
J. His friend told Rodney to break a leg!

D	inexperienced
B	describe exactly
A	a feeling of nervousness in the stomach
J	do a great job
C	have courage
E	ready to listen
I	watch carefully
F	cost a lot of money
G	hard work
H	to take a firm stand

1. picture
2. diamonds
3. stars
4. thunder
5. bird
6. mouse
7. bell
8. honey
9. monkeys
10. bee

Page 77

Answers will vary.

Page 78

Answers may vary. Possible answers include the following:
1. F
2. D
3. K
4. H
5. C
6. L
7. E
8. B
9. J
10. G
11. A
12. I

Page 79

Answers will vary.

Page 80

		Yes	No
1.	The loud <u>buzz</u> sounded as the game began.	**O**	E
2.	Greta noisily dribbled down the court.	A	**D**
3.	<u>Swish</u>! The ball slid through the net!	**B**	E
4.	The fans <u>roared</u> for the first basket.	**F**	T
5.	Both teams <u>rumbled</u> back down the court.	**C**	N
6.	Glenda quietly drove in to the basket.	H	**I**
7.	The ball <u>crashed</u> into the backboard.	**A**	Y
8.	The crowd <u>groaned</u> as the ball dropped in.	**P**	N
9.	<u>Tweet</u>! The whistle blew to stop the game.	**S**	C
10.	"There was a foul!" yelled the referee.	H	**B**
11.	Glenda's shoes <u>squeaked</u> at the line.	**G**	M
12.	The crowd was silent while Glenda shot.	T	**V**
13.	The ball hit the rim with a <u>clunk</u>.	**L**	U
14.	Then the ball bounced to the floor.	K	**W**
15.	The ball's <u>thud</u> echoed in the gym.	**J**	D

THEY CAN DUNK THEM

Page 81

Answers may vary. Possible answers include the following:
1. plop
2. crunch
3. rumble
4. slurp
5. rat a tat
6. crash
7. ring
8. bang
9. grind
10. thump
11. click
12. rustle
13. ping
14. woof

Page 82

Answers may vary. Possible answers include the following:
1. Six snazzy snakes slither along the sea at sundown.
2. Two teenage tigers tutor ten turtles in tutus.
3. The penguins ate piles of pickles after playing polo.
4. The grouchy gazelle greets its guppy guests.
5. Flocks of fancy flamingos fluff their feathers.
6. A jackrabbit juggled jars of jam in the July sun.
7. Blue bats were banging on their big banjos.
8. Ed's elk has eaten nearly everything.

Page 83

Answers will vary.

Page 84

Answers for meanings will vary.
1. Fifi's new ring is so shiny that she <u>has to wear sunglasses to look at it</u>.
2. My hamster eats so much that it <u>weighs more than a hippo</u>.
3. It is so cold outside that my fingers <u>turned into icicles</u>.
4. I can skip so fast that <u>even a cheetah can't catch me</u>.
5. My pillow is so hard I <u>dented my head</u>.
6. My brother's socks smell so bad <u>even a skunk ran away</u>.
7. The sandwich I found in my locker was so old <u>the mold was a fossil</u>.
8. My room is so messy that I <u>haven't seen my bed for two weeks</u>.
9–12. Answers will vary.

Page 87

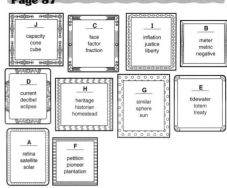

J	capacity, cone, cube
C	face, factor, fraction
I	inflation, justice, liberty
B	meter, metric, negative
D	current, decibel, eclipse
H	heritage, historian, homestead
G	similar, sphere, sun
E	tidewater, totem, treaty
A	retina, satellite, solar
F	petition, pioneer, plantation

Page 88

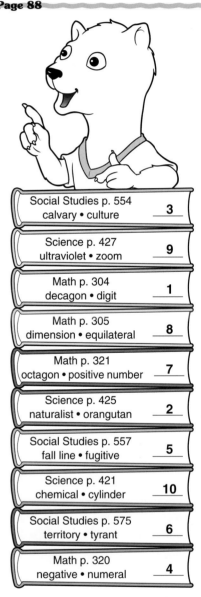

Book	Page
Social Studies p. 554 — calvary • culture	3
Science p. 427 — ultraviolet • zoom	9
Math p. 304 — decagon • digit	1
Math p. 305 — dimension • equilateral	8
Math p. 321 — octagon • positive number	7
Science p. 425 — naturalist • orangutan	2
Social Studies p. 557 — fall line • fugitive	5
Science p. 421 — chemical • cylinder	10
Social Studies p. 575 — territory • tyrant	6
Math p. 320 — negative • numeral	4

1. stigma
2. anthers
3. pollen
4. stamen
5. petals
6. tube
7. ovule
8. egg
9. seed
10. fruit

"PETAL" PUSHERS

1. beet, before, beginner
2. colt, column, comb
3. fluff, flute, flutter
4. honk, honor, hoop
5. inspect, inspire, instant
6. needle, neighbor, neon
7. pollute, polygon, poncho
8. tire, title, toad
9. wink, wiry, wisdom

1. fruit, funnel
2. blossom, bobbin
3. grow, guitar
4. orchard, orthodontics
5. seed, semester
6. pollinate, pork
7. variety, velour
8. harvest, haze
9. delicious, dependable
10. cider, civil

Yes	No
Yes	No
Yes	**No**
Yes	No
Yes	No
Yes	No
Yes	No
Yes	No
Yes	**No**
Yes	No
Yes	No
Yes	No
Yes	No
Yes	No
Yes	No
Yes	No

"RE-TAIL" STORE

arid (er'•id or ar'•id) adjective 1. Not enough water for things to live; dry and barren: *No flowers grow there because it is arid.* 2. Uninteresting or dull [Latin *arere*, to be dry] **aridity** (ər•id'•ə•tē) *noun*

1. See above.
2. 2
3. See above.
4. See above.
5. 2
6. See above.
7. aridity, noun
8. Latin
9. dry, barren, uninteresting, or dull
10. Sentences will vary.

1. parade and parallel
2. 5
3. parallel
4. Paraffin is a waxy substance used for sealing food or making candles and waxed paper.
5. Sentences will vary.
6. noun
7. Answers will vary but should include two of the following: moving in the same direction but never meeting and always being the same distance apart at all points; alike or similar; a parallel line or surface; a similarity; any of the imaginary lines on the earth's surface that are the same direction as the equator and which mark latitude.
8. 4
9. parrot
10. Sentences will vary.

1. a
2. b
3. b
4. a
5. a
6. b
7. a
8. a
9. b
10. a

1. To move one's body or feet in time to music.
2. A metal piece placed on the bottom of a shoe for tap dancing.
3. A party or gathering where people dance.
4. To strike gently.
5. To raise the foot and put it down in a new position.
6. A pounding sound or rhythm, usually in music.
7. A series of movements done in sequence while dancing or walking.
8. Certain steps done in time to music.
9. To win or defeat.

1. declare
2. carry
3. defeat
4. reduce
5. opinion
6. enjoy
7. detect
8. complete
9. leave
10. desire

Answers may vary. Possible answers include the following:

1. donate
2. pleased
3. pleasant
4. notice
5. excellent
6. joyful
7. present
8. watch
9. glad
10. fine
11. provide
12. observe

Page 103

Checkup 1

Test A	Test B
1. delay	1. rapid
2. split	2. awful
3. give	3. terrify
4. take	4. vacant
5. sell	5. steady
6. complex	6. boring
7. west	7. pass
8. straight	8. apart
9. same, different	9. below, above
10. question, answer	10. hear, ignore

Page 105

Checkup 2

Test A

1. knot
2. their
3. pair
4. You'll
5. Shane (mist) the bus this morning. missed
6. This note doesn't make (scents). sense
7. (Hour) family has two cats and a dog. Our
8. If you (eight) all of the cookies, you would be sick. ate

Test B

1. He'll
2. where
3. sweet
4. one
5. The bird flew in (threw) the open window. through
6. Chad cut the (bored) two inches too short. board
7. When is your (ant) Ellen coming to visit? aunt
8. (Right) your name at the top. Write

Page 107

Checkup 3

Test A	Test B
1. accept	1. then
2. than	2. loose
3. pitcher	3. quiet
4. clothes	4. picture
5. lay	5. good
6. already	6. close
7. chose	7. angel
8. desert	8. bring
9. set	9. except
10. good	10. all ready

Page 109

Checkup 4

Test A	Test B
1. left	1. long
2. chest	2. fan
3. check	3. story
4. b	4. b
5. a	5. a
6. a	6. a
7. b	7. c
8. c	8. b

Page 111

Checkup 5

Test A	Test B
1. rediscover	1. untidy
2. displaced	2. displeased
3. nonsense	3. substructure
4. inedible	4. indestructible
5. preview	5. recombine
6. reclaim	6. tricolor
7. impolite	7. repack
8. subsoil	8. nonrefundable
9. unsure	9. untouched
10. premade	10. subset

Page 113

Checkup 6

Test A	Test B
1. biologist	1. teacher
2. communication	2. spotless
3. penniless	3. beautiful
4. cleaner	4. organization
5. washable	5. neatly
6. delightful	6. weakness
7. kindness	7. curable
8. hungrily	8. biologist
9. scientist	9. acceptable
10. location	10. protection

Page 115

Checkup 7

Test A

1. act	4. happy
2. pay	5. digest
3. new	6. color

7. re + pay + able = able to be paid again
8. un + reason + able = not able to show reason
9. dis + agree + ment = the act of not agreeing
10. un + believe + able = not able to be believed

Test B

1. pay	4. agree
2. comfort	5. arrange
3. treat	6. break

7. non + participate + tion = the act of not participating
8. dis + respect + ful = showing lack of respect
9. un + read + able = not able to be read
10. un + like + ly = in a way that is not likely

Page 117

Checkup 8

Test A	Test B
1. calli(graph)y	1. pro(gram)
2. bi(cycle)	2. (mono)chromatic
3. (astro)nomy	3. patri(arch)
4. (photo)copier	4. (bio)psy
5. (arch)itect	5. (photo)cell
6. (thermo)stat	6. (mech)anism
7. (cycl)one	7. (thermal)
8. (hydr)aulic	8. tele(phone)
9. (aster)isk	9. (thermos)
10. atmo(sphere)	10. (grammar)
11. hemisphere	11. automobile
12. mechanic	12. recycle
13. monarch	13. symphony
14. telescope	14. asteroid
15. perimeter	15. hydrant

Page 119

Checkup 9

Test A	Test B
1. (minute)	1. in(scribe)
2. sub(scribe)	2. corrupt)
3. (fin)ish	3. (minor)
4. (manual)	4. auto(mobile)
5. de(mobil)ize	5. (fin)ale
6. inter(rupt)	6. (mani)cure
7. pre(scrip)tion	7. (audi)tory
8. (centi)pede	8. (min)us
9. (min)now	9. trans(cript)
10. (audio)	10. (ped)estal
11. diminish	11. minor
12. abrupt	12. describe
13. infinite	13. interrupt
14. manuscript	14. manager
15. centipede	15. pedometer

Page 121

Checkup 10

Test A	Test B
1. S	1. S
2. M	2. M
3. S	3. M
4. M	4. S
5. monkeys	5. bell
6. honey	6. cheetah
7. bird	7. sandpaper
8–10. Answers will vary.	8–10. Answers will vary.

Page 123

Checkup 11

Test A	Test B
1. O	1. A
2. H	2. H
3. O	3. I
4. I	4. O
5. A	5. A
6. H	6. O
7. I	7. H
8. I	8. I
9. A	9. O
10. H	10. A

Page 125

Checkup 12

Test A

> **aquarium** (ə•kwâr'•ē•əm) *noun* 1. A container, such as a tank or bowl, in which fish, other water animals, or water plants are kept: *The fish swam around the aquarium.* 2. A building where collections of fish, other water animals, and water plants are displayed: *We went to the aquarium to see the sharks.* [Latin] *noun, plural* **aquariums**

2. 4
5. 2
7. tank, bowl, or container
8. Answers will vary.

Test B

> **icy** (ī'•sē) *adjective* 1. Covered with or made of ice: *The roads were icy after the storm.* 2. Very cold: *The temperatures were icy in the winter.* 3. Cold and unfriendly: *His attitude toward her was icy.* [Middle English] *adjective* **icier, iciest**

2. 2
5. 3
7. icier, iciest
8. Answers will vary.